TOM RYCKAERT

DISRUPTIVE WORK PLACES

HOW TO CREATE YOUR SUSTAINABLE & FUTURE PROOF WORK ENVIRONMENT

Lannoo
Campus

CONTENTS

PREFACE: WHY THIS BOOK?   11

What can you expect?   11
Why me?   12

CHAPTER 1 WHERE ARE WE TODAY?   14

What is Facility Management?   15
The dimensions of workplace and Facility Management   16
The workplace through the ages   20
The Copernican revolution   21
DESTEP: Facility Management as a mirror of the outside world   25
Corporate culture: Sinek explains the difference   29
What can you expect?   32
7 steps to success   33

CHAPTER 2 DATA IS KING   34

Occupancy rate   36
What data can be used where?   38
IoT: What do your devices tell you?   40
How do you proceed?   41
Different data for different roles   42
The office as a hotel?   46
7 steps to success   47

CHAPTER 3 BETWEEN CAVEMAN AND HERD ANIMAL   48

Covid changed everything   49
Away with 'hybrid working'?   51
A new approach is required   52
Change management deserves full attention   52
Neurodiversity and design: Creating a workplace for everyone   56

Analysis, macro- and micro-planning: How do you arrange your workplace? 59
A workplace makeover 61
The workplace as a reflection of your business strategy 62
Final thoughts 66
7 Steps to success 69

CHAPTER 4 TECHNOLOGY THE ESSENTIAL BUILDING BLOCK 70

Why implement technology? 72
IWMS: The ultimate management system for Facility Managers 72
Where can you turn to? 73
What can you find in an IWMS? 74
Who benefits from IWMS? 75
CPIP: The future of IWMS 79
About smart buildings and digital twins 80
Stepping into the digital pool 82
The end goal: How was your digital day? 86
7 steps to success 87

CHAPTER 5 WITHOUT COOPERATION, THINGS WILL NOT WORK OUT 88

FM as a spider in the web 90
Know-like-trust: The step-by-step plan towards better collaboration 91
The foundations of teamwork 92
Aligning objectives: Beware of the iceberg! 93
7 steps to success 97

CHAPTER 6 HAPPY EMPLOYEES ARE HAPPY TO STAY 98

Legal framework: Preventing psychosocial risks 100
Happy employees are productive employees 104
Brain, belonging, and balance: The three dimensions of employee happiness 104
Brain: How do you get (keep) employees 'in the flow'? 105
Belonging: Building teamwork and engagement 107
A time and place for synchronous and asynchronous communication 108
Balance is essential for well-being 111
If you build it, they will work. It's not that simple 112
Corporate branding 118

A handy checklist 118
7 steps to success 119

CHAPTER 7 **SUSTAINABILITY LASTS THE LONGEST** 120

The growing importance of sustainability 122
Work to be done on sustainability 125
Calculate your ESG factor 133
The importance of FM in ESG 135
7 steps to success 141

CHAPTER 8 **THE FM SERVICE PROVIDER IN ALL ITS FACETS** 142

How did we arrive at this 'agile' approach? 144
Sharing data: Your FM service provider as a partner in excellence 145
What outsourcing model is ideal for you now? 146
The EMEA market of FM service providers in a nutshell 148
Trends in the FM service providers' market 150
A journey through the region – meet some striking FM service providers 152
Selecting FM service providers: A guide 159
Some closing thoughts 161
7 steps to success 163

CHAPTER 9 **GEN Z: NOT A CONCERN BUT A BLESSING** 165

Who are the generations in the workplace today? 166
How to keep Gen Z on board 168
Gen Z speaking 169
Gen Z at work 171
What is needed for a sustainable future-proof work environment? 175
How do we involve leadership? 175
How do we ensure lifelong learning? 175
Well-being takes centre stage 176
What have we learned from the workplace concept? 177
How does ESG fit into this story? 177
What technology do they need? 177
7 steps to success 179

CHAPTER 10 **A GLIMPSE INTO THE FUTURE**   180

The 'VUCA' world of FM   182
The office is dead! Welcome to the Metaverse   184
AI makes jobs redundant, but not people   186
Cybersecurity   188
Skills, skills, skills   191
Chief Happiness Officer   194
7 steps to success   197

CHAPTER 11 **CONCLUSION**   198

ACKNOWLEDGEMENTS   204

WHY THIS BOOK?

When I announced that I wanted to write a book about Facility Management (FM), I often received – alongside the necessary encouragement and support – the question: "Why?" This is understandable, because many books have been written about FM. But I always felt unsatisfied: either they were too theoretical, focused too much on one country or region, or highlighted only one perspective. Then I thought: "If you're so dissatisfied with the current offerings, why not do it yourself?"

Indeed, I had several clear ambitions for the book. I wanted to provide space for universal issues linked to FM and the workplace. I wanted a book that does not stop at a physical border between two countries but offers examples from all over Europe and the Middle East. It had to be a practical and relatable book, which is why I collected a lot of use cases. And that's what this book is really about: sharing knowledge and experience, not just from myself but directly from the market. And look, two years later, the result is on the shelves of bookstores and now also with you, dear reader. This practically conceived guide, with a clear step-by-step plan and lots of concrete tips and stories for you as a reader to reflect on, can, I hope, inform and also inspire you. After reading, you should be able to create (even) more impact within your company.

WHAT CAN YOU EXPECT?

This book is not only aimed at Facility Managers but at everyone who – especially with the new approach to FM in today's workplace – deals with the subject from near or from afar. The speed at which changes have come upon us is unprecedented. It's about the 'disruptive' (disrupted) workplace itself as well as the many disruptions that have and will continue to have an impact on our workplace in the future. But above all, this book is a guide to help you create a sustainable and future-proof work environment.

The focus is on providing a practice-oriented approach across the various topics you deal with today. And what better way to do this than with state-of-the-art use cases and by letting market experts speak? In most of the conversations I've had for this book, the same questions kept coming up: "Does hybrid working really work? I want to see how I can set this up at my company." "Technology: is too complex for me, I've never seen it work anywhere." "What more can I do for sustainability than make my vehicle fleet electric?" "How can I use my FM Service Provider in a more flexible way?" "I want to approach FM strategically, but how do I get a seat at the director's table?" And so on.

Well, in this book, you will find the answers.

Allow me to start with a disclaimer. In this book, we mainly deal with the corporate working environment, the traditional office environment. Well, traditional might not be the best-chosen word, as we will discuss how strongly that workplace is subject to change. But it's important to realise that we are starting from such a work environment. I am aware that, for example, an industrial environment and a hospital environment differ significantly from an average office environment, and they perhaps deserve their own book. At the same time, I am convinced that a number of the factors we discuss here can also be applicable to those other environments.

WHY ME?

Why did I feel called to write this book? How did I actually end up in the field of FM and the workplace environment? I sometimes wonder myself, but one thing is for sure: by now, it's not so much a job or a sector for me, but a real passion. I always wonder how I can add value to 'my' beloved sector. More than 20 years ago, the head of the Facility Management programme at Odisee University College came to give an information session at my high school. My friend Michel Liessens and I found this interesting. It was varied and seemed to offer different perspectives for a future job. The earlier ambitions to follow a marketing education were discarded, and I chose an FM education.

Explaining this to my family and friends at the time was quite a challenge. "What are you studying now? What will you do with that?" I always had a standard answer ready: "Imagine a car factory; what is their core process? Producing cars, indeed. Well, FM is everything surrounding it that helps to support this core process. Taking care of the building, maintenance, cleaning, catering, etc., so that others can focus on producing cars." People then nodded eagerly, but didn't go further into it. All this was seen as a given.

In the meantime, I have built a beautiful career and had the luxury of being able to work at quite a few international companies. You will also notice my love for technology and innovation in the book, partly stemming from my professional years at some market leaders in the integrated workplace management system (IWMS) market. Here, I also learned to align software and processes, and especially to dare to question existing processes. This has shaped my process thinking and project-based approach to what it is today.

In addition, I spent a significant part of my career at an FM service provider, Facilicom, and this is probably where I learned the most, with special thanks to Claudine Decorte, who was my manager for almost 15 years. She taught me a no-nonsense approach where the customer always comes first. When she couldn't go to a commercial appointment once, I was asked if I could take over. I did this with pleasure and thus ended up in the commercial field, and immediately felt at home. I love it. Every day is different; you visit so many diverse companies and try to match the right facility solution to them.

During the writing of this book, I was active at PROCOS Group. Here, the world of workplace strategy and design – an essential part of how we deal with our workplace environment – opened up further for me. In March 2023, my wife Kathleen Louckx and I founded our own consultancy and advisory firm, 2nRich. We focus on enriching yourself, your team, and your organisation through training, workshops, and coaching sessions, always with an eye on 'happiness' and well-being in the workplace. Kathleen's passion is in work happiness, from an HR perspective. I have learned a lot from her and been able to apply that knowledge. I write this book from our company as part of our ambition to contribute by sharing knowledge, alongside keynotes, workshops, and strategic guidance for companies in their facility and workplace challenges.

Professional associations play an important role in elevating the maturity of the field to the next level. Since the beginning of my career, I have always been fond of IFMA (International Facility Management Association). They are the world's largest and most recognised association for Facility Management professionals. Through my engagement, I am a board member at the IFMA Belgium Chapter, responsible for marketing and communication, as well as being the technology and innovation lead. The FM community in Belgium is powerful in itself, but you really benefit from the global IFMA network when you can share knowledge and experiences with countless like-minded people around the world. With my experience and network, I set to work, and this practical guide came into being. I am convinced that everyone will find tips and tricks in it. I wish you much reading pleasure!

CHAPTER 1

WHERE ARE WE TODAY?

To start our journey together in creating a sustainable and future-proof work environment, it is worth outlining the current situation and the challenges the market is facing. Throughout my career, I have never seen so many changes in the way we work happen in such a short period. And this, of course, means that you have to approach the management of it, Facility Management (FM), in a new way. In this chapter, you will notice that I have spoken with various market leaders to hear their vision on how they view FM and the workplace environment, now and in the future. They are on the front line every day in their region and are, in my opinion, ideal discussion partners. Furthermore, we will define FM, get to work with the 4 Ps of the work environment, delve into history, and see how we need to consider external factors to better frame FM. And we will briefly examine corporate culture because the workplace environment will contribute to how your company is perceived.

WHAT IS FACILITY MANAGEMENT?

Since it pays little to reinvent the wheel, I like to refer to the definition set by IFMA (International Facility Management Association), the world's largest professional organisation for Facility Managers (see box). In this book, we will generally use the abbreviation 'FM' when referring to Facility Management.

> **IFMA's definition of Facility Management**
>
> "Facility or facilities management (FM) is a profession dedicated to supporting people. It ensures the functionality, comfort, safety, sustainability, and efficiency of the built environment – the buildings we live and work in and their surrounding infrastructure. As defined by ISO (International Organization for Standardization) and adopted by IFMA: "FM is an organisational function which integrates people, place, and process within the built environment with the purpose of improving the quality of life of people and the productivity of the core business."

The mention of ISO is noteworthy in this definition. When an ISO standard is developed for a discipline, it certainly means it is a crucial part of any comprehensive corporate policy. The standard 'ISO 41011:2017 – FM' not only illustrates the importance of FM but also suggests that it is a field with complex interactions and procedures – a suspicion that is, of course, entirely justified. The definition also refers to the built environment and places; in this book, we will focus on the workplace and work environment in a 'corporate office' environment. Naturally, many things are also applicable to other sectors and environments. The facility manager has the important task of contributing to the workplace and the environment. He/she is central and can create an impact on a multitude of domains, as you will see in the illustration below.

Figure 1.1: The facility manager is central.

THE DIMENSIONS OF WORKPLACE AND FACILITY MANAGEMENT (ALSO KNOWN AS THE 4 Ps)

In discussing all facets of the workplace and FM, the so-called 3 Bs (bricks, bytes, behaviour) have been used since the rise of 'The New Way of Working', to which 2 Bs (balance and belonging) and 1 S (sustainability) were later added. Because we're talking about the 'disruptive workplace' in this book, where literally everything is questioned, I've also allowed myself to trade these 5 Bs for a new set of letters, namely the 4 Ps. This, in my opinion, best sums up the different dimensions of FM.

They stand for:

PEOPLE

This is mainly about the 'workplace experience' – how employees experience the workplace. This is not just a rational story of how our behaviours are influenced by the workplace, but also an emotional one: you want to create a work environment that appeals to the hearts of employees and gives them a sense of belonging. But you also want to offer a good overall experience, where the balance between home and office work is optimally respected, where collaboration between colleagues and between generations is supported as well as possible, and more. In short: you want to create a work environment where employees can feel happy.

PLACES

Here, I refer to the different physical workplaces – in the office, on the move, at home etc., the buildings and their surroundings, and the services that FM provides to manage and maintain these buildings.

PERFORMANCE

Not only are the buildings themselves central, but also aspects of the workplace that contribute to employees being able to function optimally. In this book, I will, for example, go into detail on the role of software and technology: how they contribute to better management of the workplace on the one hand, but also how they make those workplaces more efficient to use by employees on the other.

PLANET

Also, the last P is getting an increasingly prominent role in FM. Buildings must be made as energy-efficient as possible. Not just for the lower energy bill, but also because sustainability and environmentally conscious action are increasingly at the top of the priority list in corporate strategy. And not only to focus on the E (energy) of ESG, we will also approach the other themes. How can it have an impact on social issues, diversity, inclusion, and equality?

The icons will be used later in the chapter to indicate where the focus lies in the various topics covered.

LARA PAEMEN

Managing Director of IFMA (International Facility Management Association) EMEA.

"As the head of IFMA's entire EMEA region, I notice daily that even within Europe, it's difficult to speak of a homogeneous FM landscape. Non-Europeans sometimes find it hard to understand, but the diversity within this one region is immense. Each country has its culture and education level, and this has a deep impact on their FM reality. So, there isn't one overarching FM for Europe. However, you can distinguish some homogeneous regions within Europe. In the Nordics, much attention is paid to well-being, soft services, the experience of the work environment. In Eastern Europe, there's a strong focus on BIM (Building Information Modeling) and other forms of digitalisation. For example, in the Czech Republic, all new government buildings must be made in BIM. In Southern Europe, the emphasis is on technical aspects, on operations and maintenance. Only companies with an international focus are strategy-oriented there. It's a less mature market, although there are young startups in prop tech in Spain that are betting on this. The Benelux region, finally, is strongly influenced by the Nordics, but also remains very technical and sometimes misses the boat in certain areas.

The past years, the pandemic and the resulting 'agile' way of working have questioned many certainties. How many square metres do you need, and how do you use them? How do you serve your employees when they're not in the office? How do you make the workplace attractive for current and new employees? What needs does Generation Z have, and how do you address them? Also, the increasing digitalisation of buildings, assets, and more forces the FMer to retrain and redefine the job. Attention must also be paid to cybersecurity, for the more you digitalise, the greater the chance of leaks and breaches. Risk analysis becomes a full part of FM: weighing the cyber danger against the possibilities that digitalisation offers.

Facility Managers may well be a bit less modest when it comes to their contribution to the company's ESG strategy. FM plays an important role here, and you should not let yourself be cornered into the technical and operational. Strategically positioning FM will also contribute to the profession's appeal. Professional associations have a significant role to play in this. The old infrastructure poses many challenges in terms of sustainability, and it is often easier to opt for new infrastructure. But countries like Italy, with a rich past and heritage, are not in favour of this. This is a delicate balance where the government will have to play a big role, – but also professional organisations like IFMA, especially in finding innovative solutions. Here, we must learn to look at other countries and regions, so we don't always start from scratch.

build a work environment to which employees wish to return. The old FM is dead; long live the new FM. This new FM is driven by disruptive technology, forcing us to look at things differently. The operational will largely be automated, giving the FMer more time for analysis and the experience factor. For this, we will also need training and new talents. Facility manager, be the monkey on the rock. Tell your stories, make your impact clear. This way, you can claim your rightful place in the organisation. We as a professional association are happy to contribute to this awareness that FM is a true pillar of the organisation."

"BE THE MONKEY ON THE ROCK"

In Southern and Eastern Europe, the return to the office is almost complete. In other regions, it's not moving that fast. The most important thing is not to impose it but to

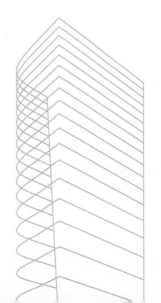

THE WORKPLACE THROUGH THE AGES

To understand why the current changes in FM are called 'disruptive' and revolutionary, we must look back at how the workplace was considered and managed in the past. Not only does this put everything into perspective, but it also helps avoid repeating past mistakes. Therefore, I invite you to look back with me before we resolutely turn our gaze forward. From ancient times through the Middle Ages to today, the work environment has always played an important role in our society. Of course, the workplace has evolved over the centuries. Especially during the Industrial Revolution, in the 18th and 19th centuries, we saw the first significant change. Large factories were built to enable production at scale, with hundreds or thousands of workers in the same building. With the arrival of these large factories in growing cities, there was also an increasing need for efficient management of these industrial buildings. In response, 'plant engineers' and 'factory supervisors' appeared on the scene: they had to ensure smooth operation on the work floor, but also maintenance and safety in the workplace.

The attention to the worker as a person was still limited then. They were mainly seen as a pawn in production, not so much as a full person. Also, for office or knowledge work, which claimed its place in the wake of factories, we saw the same attitude. The focus was on maintenance and upkeep of buildings. Even though there was somewhat more attention paid to the well-being of office workers, the focus was largely on productivity and efficiency, and on the human as a link in the big network. This then shifted more towards other services such as cleaning, catering, and security, to create an ideal work environment for the employees.

With the arrival of trade unions and other organisations, that well-being received more attention – companies had to respond to keep employees satisfied. This was reflected in FM: in addition to the focus on technical support, there was also more attention to the workplace as a healthy environment that promotes the well-being of employees. At the same time, we see office environments changing into often large office landscapes with a tendency towards uniformity: everyone has the same desk, chair, and working tools. Later, we learned that everyone is different and that there are various types of activities. Meanwhile, a whole (r)evolution has been effected within the work environment. You need to be able to do concentrated work, bring your colleagues together for meetings, have lunch together at noon etc. very diverse activities, and thus other types of offices with a diverse environment that offered space for these different activities emerged.

But it could be better: by examining all the tasks that need to be done and aligning the workplace environment accordingly, companies could make their buildings contribute to the efficiency and satisfaction of employees. This approach to the workplace, known as 'activity-based working', originated in the period between 2008 and 2010. It was thought out for the individual and employees: What do they need to do their job? In the period between 2020 and 2023, the next shift came, towards hybrid working, adding an extra dimension to the workplace. We now also work place – and time – independent. A serious challenge for the Facility Manager and the workplace, as you will discover further on in this book!

THE COPERNICAN REVOLUTION

Everything changes; it has never been otherwise. But the speed and impact of change have never been as great as in the past three decades.
It started with **the advent of the internet**. In three steps, this irrevocably changed our lives and our way of working:

- Web 1: in the first period (1991–2004), the internet was mainly a static environment and (inexhaustible) source of information.
- Web 2: from 2004, social media appeared, gradually turning the internet into a highway with two-way traffic.
- Web 3: in recent years, the semantic web has emerged, and it will play a key role in current and future FM: the increased connectivity that makes remote work easier, the concept of the 'digital twin' as a virtual lab for experiments, artificial intelligence that makes our buildings 'smart buildings' etc. These and other technological breakthroughs will be discussed in detail in the following chapters.

The financial crisis (which began in 2008) also had a huge impact on FM. Companies were forced to reduce costs and optimise management, including with the help of technology. Unfortunately, this reflex to save costs has never disappeared. There was a strong focus on outsourcing, at many levels. And there was more attention than ever before to energy management: consumption was scrutinised, and alternative energy sources increasingly appeared as a healthy business choice. The importance of risk management also became glaringly clear; some risks turned out to be not so imaginary after all.

Think of the most recent unexpected twists that have hit us: the Covid pandemic, the war in Ukraine, the energy crisis, and the war in Gaza. The most impactful was probably the Covid pandemic, which made us think about the well-being of employees and a healthy work environment, but also about daily activities such as cleaning buildings. The war in Ukraine and the associated energy crisis and economic recession led to a renewed focus on cost reduction but also on sustainable and environmentally-conscious building management, which in turn requires new investments. A complicated balancing act.

The rise in wages is certainly a point to include in these 'challenges'. Since FM is a people business, this has a significant impact on the cost. This will force Facility Managers to look differently at how they make up their budgets and which services they wish to contract. For an FM service provider, this has an impact on their ongoing contracts, where costs increase and they cannot pass on all wage costs (indexations) 1 to 1. Efficiency in operational service delivery will play a crucial role here.

These and other challenges are also addressed in the boxes you will find scattered throughout this chapter. Each box offers a different perspective, presenting one-to-one vision of the trends and challenges that FM faces today. In summary, there have never been so many profound changes coming at us at such a high speed. They have all made us aware that we need to and can approach things differently. This conclusion also applies to FM and the workplace in general. The workplace has become a 'disruptive workplace', where nothing goes as it used to. All these changes for FM in Europe and the Middle East will be discussed one by one in the following chapters.

MARK WHITTAKER

IWFM (Institute of Workplace and Facilities Management) chair.

ANDREW HULBERT

IWFM (Institute of Workplace and Facilities Management) deputy chair.

Mark: "Ten years ago, hardly anyone knew what FM was. That changed after the fire in London's Grenfell Tower and even more when Covid shook everything up: suddenly, safety and health became top of mind, and it was expected that FM would embrace and apply the stricter recommendations around it."

Andrew: "Finding the necessary talent remains the biggest challenge. Most people stumble into it by accident. We already have two university programmes and many colleges that teach FM, but even with that, we're not there yet. That's one of the biggest challenges for our sector."

Mark: "There's a general 'war for talent' going on. And FM plays a big role in this: on the one hand, you have to create an environment where it's pleasant to work, and on the other hand, you have to realise that employees won't come every day, and you have to adjust your FM accordingly. The work-life balance determines our agenda more than ever. It's no coincidence that 'work from home' is the most searched term in job listings today."

Andrew: "Facility and workplace management are no longer about the buildings but about the experience. How can we make the office more interesting? A 3D printing room? A cinema? An after-work bar? You also have to take into account the changing behaviour in London. Mondays and Fridays are very quiet in London offices, and Thursday is the new Friday. This has a major impact on the strategy around needed space. Many lease contracts are made so that one can quickly (literally) 'downsize' and engage other services."

Mark: "For IWFM, it's important to elevate FM to a strategic level, even though the budget pressure and its impact on FM and the workplace are tremendous."

"THURSDAY IS THE NEW FRIDAY IN LONDON OFFICES"

Andrew: "The focus is on information sharing, training, and certifications. If we can get our 13,000 members to a high certification level, the whole sector will benefit from it."

Mark: "Companies want more sustainable buildings. Not just out of ideological conviction but also to make the brand and company more attractive to customers, candidates, and their own employees."

Andrew: "Not every old building can be made sustainable; some are better

completely demolished to start over from scratch."

Mark: "Technology will be high on the priority list for every FM and workplace manager in the coming years. Companies also see IoT, AI, and robotics as a solution to the lack of available talent. CAFM (Computer Aided Facility Management) will be important in supporting daily FM activities, but that will take time. BIM has been high on the agenda for ten years and still needs to fully mature."

Andrew: "I also see a lot of attention in the near future to the work environment as an extension of the home environment: you need to offer an environment where it's pleasant to come together. Everyone misses the stories told at the coffee machine."

Mark: "Our FM community urgently needs to go to schools to get students excited about facility and workplace management. Not just colleges and universities but also secondary schools. The younger they feel involved in the issues, the better."

Andrew: "At the same time, FM must be brought to the boardroom level. After all, we are determining the workplace of the future, and thus also what it feels like to work there. That's more than an operational task; it requires strategy and entrepreneurship. We, as the FM community, may well trumpet that a bit more often."

DESTEP: FACILITY MANAGEMENT AS A MIRROR OF THE OUTSIDE WORLD

FM is not an island. Further into this book, we will go into this statement in detail. We will then look at how the Facility Manager must strive for a good relationship with all other departments to be able to perform optimally. However, here I also want to emphasise the connection between FM and the outside world, the reality around us that influences corporate operations and thus also workplace strategy. To get a grip on this complex dynamic, I like to use the DESTEP approach, visually displayed in the diagram below.

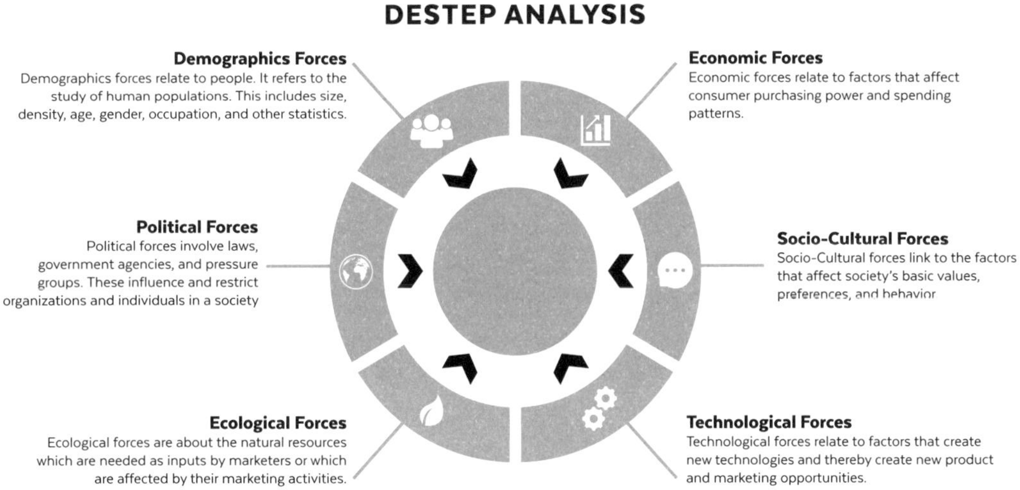
DESTEP ANALYSIS
Demographics Forces
Demographics forces relate to people. It refers to the study of human populations. This includes size, density, age, gender, occupation, and other statistics.
Economic Forces
Economic forces relate to factors that affect consumer purchasing power and spending patterns.
Political Forces
Political forces involve laws, government agencies, and pressure groups. These influence and restrict organizations and individuals in a society
Socio-Cultural Forces
Socio-Cultural forces link to the factors that affect society's basic values, preferences, and behavior
Ecological Forces
Ecological forces are about the natural resources which are needed as inputs by marketers or which are affected by their marketing activities.
Technological Forces
Technological forces relate to factors that create new technologies and thereby create new product and marketing opportunities.

Figure 1.2: DESTEP applied to FM.

DESTEP is an acronym that stands for Demographic, Economic, Socio-cultural, Technological, Ecological, and Political/legal; in short, for all factors that influence and even determine the environment of a company. In this book, I limit myself to the regions I am familiar with, namely Europe and the Middle East. And, even though there are many similarities within and between these regions, we also see significant differences from region to region and from country to country. Anyone who has a good understanding of a company's external environment can effectively use the opportunities and avoid the threats associated with the country(scape) in which the company operates. If a company sets its strategic policy based on the findings of a DESTEP analysis, it's taking a good step forward towards success in its environment. For the workplace environment and FM, this analysis can also be very useful. For this book, it means that, thanks to DESTEP, we better understand the concrete context of a company and thus can also better assess needs and opportunities. For FM, too, there are many similarities between companies in these regions, but certainly also many differences. This will become apparent from the many use cases throughout this book.

Here are some examples:

- **Demographic:** 'love for talent'. How can you optimally fill your FM team (both internally and externally)? Not an easy task with an aging population and an acute shortage of technical profiles.
- **Economic:** the economic recession is leading to a lot of investments being postponed. At the same time, it's high time to invest in sustainability and a future-proof workplace policy and concept. You have to invest in time to stay ahead of the competition. But how do you reconcile this with the brake that most companies still apply to investments?
- **Socio-cultural:** Each country and region has its culture and peculiarities. This has a significant impact on the maturity level of FM: it varies enormously from country to country.
- **Technological:** 'smart buildings' are popping up like mushrooms. What is the impact of this complex matter for FM?
- **Ecological:** ESG (Environmental, Social, Governance) and SDGs (Sustainable Development Goals) are at the top of every company and FM agenda. How do you approach this concretely?
- **Political:** What guidelines and legislation do local politics provide to tackle the above issues? How can you easily renovate and make buildings sustainable? A big task, which differs per country and often involves long and difficult processes.

ALI ALSUWAIDI

Vice President of MEFMA (Middle East Facility Management Association).

"In the Middle East, FM is already quite well-established and mature. But workplace management is still somewhat neglected. It's usually pushed to HR, and taken over by real estate managers or investors. There's little interaction between the two disciplines, even though they really should be seen together. Governments and international companies see the importance of interaction and employee well-being, but most companies still have a long way to go. That's one of the big challenges for MEFMA: as a professional organisation, we want to raise awareness about this. As vice president of MEFMA, I help close the gap in FM in this region. We talk to the various stakeholders in this sector and work on awareness, education, and development of people in this sector, with workshops, training, award ceremonies, and conferences, where experiences and use cases are shared, also with FM organisations from other countries. We are now beginning to reap the benefits.

Last year, we saw a lot of marketing and focus on awareness in the FM sector in this region. Covid has had an impact on how FM is viewed, but there's no 'disruptive' trend yet. However, you do notice a lot of effort and interest in using technology for better FM, both from the customer and the suppliers. They're looking at how technology and data can lead to better decisions. One important condition for this seems to be the use of an 'open protocol', allowing all parties involved to share data and information more easily. All major suppliers must learn to cooperate to make better buildings possible. Machine learning can also play a big role in this.

In the next three to five years, I see an explosion of data from all possible players in this sector. Among other things, in our pursuit of energy efficiency and sustainability, technologies such as IoT and machine learning will play a crucial role. They will help us question environmentally-friendly 'over design', the trend where some real estate players provide overly intensive installations for cooling and air conditioning in their rush to get a building ready as quickly as possible, with many consequences on energy consumption and maintenance.

My tip for the FM community? Go for sustainable, and employee-friendly. Keep a close eye on new technologies, but don't forget the people. We will always need a lot of talent, so invest not only in recruitment but also and especially in the training and development of your talent."

"I ADVOCATE FOR AN OPEN PROTOCOL SO THAT ALL MAJOR PLAYERS CAN COOPERATE BETTER."

CORPORATE CULTURE: SINEK EXPLAINS THE DIFFERENCE

Of course, FM is not just the product of external factors. The company's own factors also largely determine the business strategy and approach around it. In other words: the culture of the company also plays a big role.

To describe the interaction between FM and corporate culture, I like to refer to Simon Sinek's Golden Circle, with his Why, How and What approach.

Figure 1.3: Simon Sinek's Golden Circle.

Applied to FM, this sounds roughly as follows:

Why?
We want to create a sustainable and future-oriented work environment where our people are happy and can perform their job as efficiently as possible.

How?
We will develop a policy in the short, medium, and long term that includes all factors related to the workplace. This results in an optimisation of workplaces and a streamlined facility service.

What?
We will develop a workplace strategy and analyse the current real estate portfolio, introducing 'activity-based working' or 'event-based working' where we can work place and time independent (hybrid working). The main message here is that FM must be closely integrated with the general strategy and business operations. Otherwise, you risk ending up with building and workplace management that is not aligned with the specific needs and expectations of the company and its employees, and that is not supported by top management as it should be.

NATALIE HOFMAN

Chair of EuroFM.

"The Netherlands has been at the forefront of FM for a long time. There were many FM programmes, at colleges and universities, and partly because of that, a decent influx. This also led to the necessary maturity, with useful theoretical FM models and outsourcing models. Even though we're falling back a bit from our leading role, we're still ahead in Europe. Originally, the Facility Manager was a 'doer'. We see a problem, and we tackle it. Nowadays, the human factor has been added: what does the employee need from FM? Finally, the role of technology in general and IT in particular has increased enormously. The link with IT is undeniable and we have to deal with it.

The Facility Manager must actually be a kind of hyper-social ITer.

Aligning the workplace with the needs and impact of the employee is not an easy task – one with which we continue to struggle. Today, we see a gradual return to the offices and a rethinking of the office towards a meeting place. But what does this mean, for example, for the prevailing parking norms and who we consider as a 'visitor'? What is the ideal way of working in 2024? How will 'co-working' spaces develop further? Is this still financially appealing? And where do we get the answer to all these questions? This can be a huge opportunity for advisors and consultancy.

Making the step towards sustainability is less straightforward than you might think. Much of the old and less sustainable infrastructure is in the hands of small and medium-sized enterprises, which do not always have the budget to achieve sustainability goals. Moreover, you also have to make the distinction between owners and tenants of a building. Owners feel less pressure to make the building as sustainable as possible. As tenants, we're not taking a strong stance to move to a more sustainable building. On the positive side, we have built a good working digital network within Europe, which ensures good cooperation.

The new way of working leads to a mix of work environments next to each other, with the digital platform overarching everything. This requires a new corporate culture: what do you stand for as an organisation, and what does this mean for the service you provide to your employees? The typical 9-to-5 approach doesn't work anymore, but what does this mean for FM? If you want to dine with the team in the evening, today you have no choice but to look for a restaurant outside. Perhaps the FM of tomorrow can provide an answer to this?

"A FACILITY MANAGER MUST BE A KIND OF HYPER-SOCIAL COMPUTER SCIENTIST"

If the Facility Manager continues to be associated with operational services such as cleaning and catering, I see the term disappearing in favour of, for example, WEX (Workplace Experience) Manager. There's so much

more involved in today's work experience: working from home and making chairs and IT hardware available for this; emergency plans in case, for example, the internet goes down for a month; mobility and (un)availability of public transport etc. Again, we are 'doers' and tackle all these problems. Only the problems are totally different from a few years ago. And we haven't even touched on the impact of climate change yet. I wonder if our companies will be able to achieve the sustainability policy purely from intrinsic motivation and corporate conviction. We all want to do the right thing, but as soon as it has concrete consequences, we often look at it differently. Look at how we all got back on planes, despite all the awareness around the environmental impact. I do wonder if we'll manage this task without strict rules and enforcement."

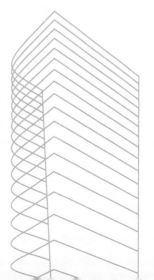

WHAT CAN YOU EXPECT?

Within the workplace environment, there are various dimensions and facets that deserve our attention. So we'll explore the importance and utility of data for today's facility manager in chapter 2. We study the evolution of the workplace as a reflection of the social needs of the employee in chapter 3. Chapter 4 is dedicated to technology, and the different levels at which it can contribute to a better workplace and more efficient FM. Chapter 5 is devoted to the importance of collaboration as the engine of the company, and how FM can make better collaboration possible. In chapter 6, we discuss how the well-being and happiness of employees deserve attention, as an important asset for retention within the company. Chapter 7 describes how sustainability and ESG (Environmental, Social and Governance) are playing an increasingly large role in FM. Chapter 8 describes the different models of FM as a service. Gen Z, the digital natives, also influence today's workplace; you'll discover how exactly in chapter 9. And as a finale, chapter 10 offers you a glimpse into the future: what can we expect in the coming years in terms of FM and workplace experience? All the chapters together offer you a deep and multifaceted insight into what we mean by the 'disruptive workplace'. And hopefully, also some handles to make your own FM and workplace more efficient, productive, and pleasant than ever before.

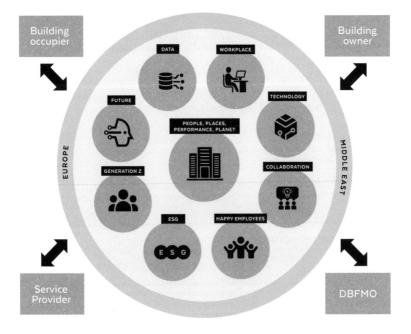

Figure 1.4: Visual representation of book content.

7 STEPS TO SUCCESS

All subsequent chapters will conclude with '7 steps to success'. Herein, I sum-marise the most important steps of the chapter as a guideline for you, the reader: if you take these seven steps into account, the chance of success is much greater. For this first, introductory chapter, there's only one 'step to success', and you've actually already taken it: by reading this book, you get a broad and deep overview of the disruptive workplace and what it means for the profession of FM. The only step towards success I can recommend here is: keep reading, so I can share all these insights with you!

I wish you a lot of reading pleasure!

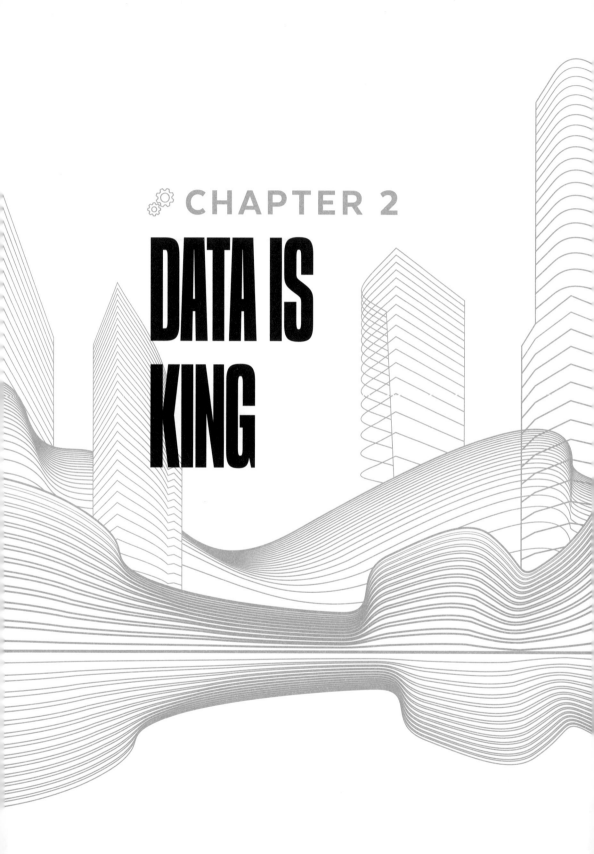

CHAPTER 2

DATA IS KING

"To measure is to know."
"Data is king."
"Knowledge is power."

There are enough slogans to emphasise the importance of data in our current economy and society. But fortunately, behind those slogans lie very concrete benefits. Indeed, data make a difference in many cases, including FM. As 'smart buildings' and their configurations generate more and more data, there is increasingly more to measure. And those who measure more also know more. However, not all data lead to new insights. The following diagram explains what I mean. To transform data into useful information, you need structure and context. To turn that information into knowledge, you must understand the why behind the information and give meaning to that information. Knowledge leads to wisdom when it offers you insights into how to achieve better results. And that wisdom then leads to the right decisions. The journey from data to good decisions is long but definitely worth it.

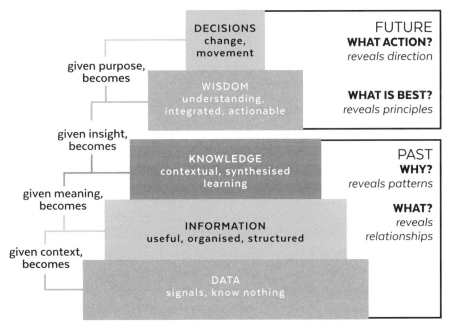

Figure 2.1: The journey from data to good decisions.

It might become clearer with an example. Suppose your HVAC (Heating Venti-lation and Cooling) system indicates that the temperature remains unusually high in a specific meeting room (data); this teaches you that the meeting room is overheated for a large part of the time (information). A technician's onsite in-vestigation determines that the thermostat in the room is defective (knowledge). A new sensor system is then installed to provide an error message if the sensor stops working, in order to avoid such malfunctions in the future. Thus, we gain wisdom and can make thoughtful decisions. And, importantly: not all data are useful, and certainly not for every purpose. Measuring for the sake of measuring has no added value. Converting the right data into useful insights, which can be acted upon: that's what it's all about. Therefore, we should start with this ques-tion: What do we, as Facility Managers, want to measure? What information do we need or can help us in our job? Which data lead us to better insights and more thoughtful decisions?

I can already tell you what we will not measure. The 'total building life cycle' starts with architecture and design, then moves to the construction phase, and when the building is fully completed, we enter the operational phase. In each of these phases, data are measured and collected today. It goes without saying that Facility Managers are particularly interested in the last, operational, phase. But it quickly becomes clear that even here, more than enough data are available. We have in-deed passed the era where the Facility Manager had to continuously walk around the buildings they managed to know what was happening. Nowadays, the for-ward-looking Facility Manager still keeps in touch with the workplace, but is also supported by data collected from the building, the building owner, the company's employees, and service providers.

OCCUPANCY RATE

The first data we examine do not concern the building itself as much as the em-ployees who inhabit it. Specifically, the occupancy rate - the percentage of employ-ees present during office hours - provides very useful data. The trend of using oc-cupancy rate as input in striving towards data-driven service had already started, but it completely broke through during the Covid pandemic: this was when atten-tion to remote and hybrid work exploded. Many companies are seeking the right balance between home and office work, but every Facility Manager worldwide can confirm that this irreversible trend has a significant impact on building occu-pancy rates. Before the pandemic, the occupancy rate over a year was 70 to 80%; today it is considerably lower. How much exactly is hard to quantify and varies greatly by country and sector. However, there are some general trends to observe. On average, employees work from home 1 to 2 days a week. Here, we also notice a marked 'camel effect' in office presence, with peaks on Tuesday and Thursday, and a lower occupancy on the other days, as illustrated below. Employees prefer coming to the office on these days rather than on Monday or Friday, which are also more commonly taken as days off, or on Wednesday, when childcare often plays a role in the choice of workplace.

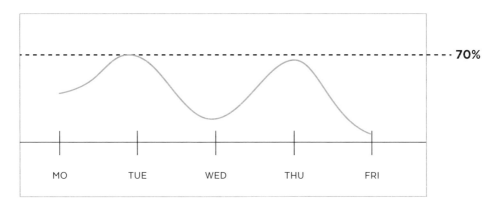

Figure 2.2: Post Covid occupancy rate – source Facile by PROCOS Group.

Meanwhile, numerous international companies are rigorously scaling back remote work and in some top companies – with Tesla and X as the most notable examples – remote working is being abolished entirely. But even then, hybrid working remains an undeniable reality, with an estimated average occupancy rate of 30 to 40% in corporate office environments and where workplace optimisation has not yet been implemented. But to use this data on the occupancy of corporate buildings effectively, for example, to optimise the services you offer in the workplace environment, you also need other data – data that tell you something about employee satisfaction and well-being at home and in the office, for example. Looking at the Leesman Index and the satisfaction of employees with their home workplace compared to their office workplace, we see a significant difference (see box). It is a challenge for the Facility Manager to bridge the gap!

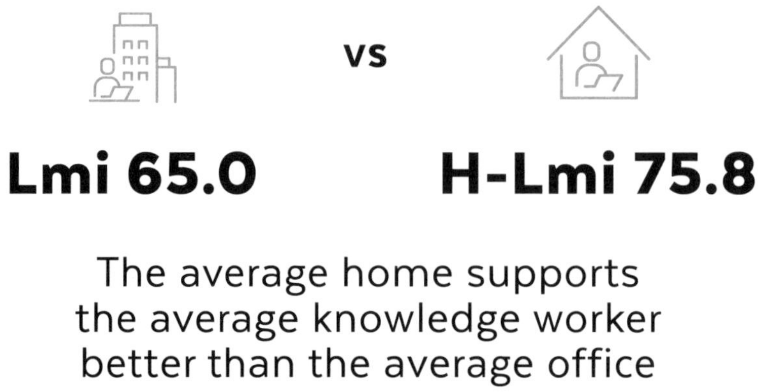

 VS

Lmi 65.0   H-Lmi 75.8

The average home supports the average knowledge worker better than the average office

Figure 2.3: Employee satisfaction at home & office workplace – Leesman: the workplace reset report 2023.

WHAT DATA CAN BE USED WHERE?

Now that the different perspectives and potential data stakeholders are known, we can delve into more detail on which data can be useful at what level and at what moment.

In the **workplace**, besides occupancy rates, data that determine employee well-being and comfort play a major role. Temperature, CO_2 levels, humidity, light intensity (measured in lux), and noise (in decibels) etc. All these data can be measured and utilised to improve employee well-being in the office.

In the **home workplace**, Microsoft Teams will become an especially important source of data. Microsoft remains the de facto standard for collaboration and productivity software, and this platform can tell us a lot about how and when employees collaborate on it. And when the 'Places' feature becomes available, creating virtual workspaces and managing real workplaces, it, along with Teams, will become an extremely valuable information source for the Facility Manager.

For specific types of service delivery, which we typically call 'Agile service delivery', different kinds of data can be useful. For **cleaning services**, for example, the schedule can be tailored to the building's occupancy rate. The more insight they have into the occupancy of offices and meeting rooms, the better they can provide their services without causing any inconvenience. This can make a significant difference in employees' experience and their judgement of the service quality. Other useful data include so-called 'smart toilets', which monitor consumption of soap, towel rolls, toilet paper etc. This allows for optimising available supplies, although this has real added value only for larger office buildings. Reception and security services obviously benefit from insights into the occupancy rate as well. But they also benefit from data from 'visitor management tools', which teach them when more or fewer visitors are typically present. This way, they can tailor their available staff to this.

For **building management** itself, data from the BMS (Building Management System) are particularly useful. This data tells you a lot about the use of installations and assets, allowing for optimised maintenance and interventions. Previously, analysing these data was entirely manual, but nowadays there are many 'smart' BMS that can automatically make recommendations and optimise processes using algorithms and Artificial Intelligence (AI). Regulating the ideal environment – in terms of temperature, humidity and CO_2 – and optimising energy and water consumption can also be largely automated based on this data. A significant advantage for the future, as water and other resources become increasingly scarce.

Last but not least: if you want to tailor the office environment to the needs and expectations of employees, data on employee satisfaction also become a crucial source of information. Anyone aiming to develop the ideal office concept should indeed seek relevant data. A satisfaction survey might be the best source of information. However, as a general overview, the following data from Leesman's report on average employee satisfaction across several key aspects and services can be utilised. It shows that the company restaurant and the room reservation system still appeal to just over half of the employees, but there is much less overall satisfaction with the noise level and temperature. A good starting point for those looking for areas of improvement, I believe. In both cases, it involves a personal perception, making it harder to provide the perfect solution for everyone. However, there are general areas of improvement that can lead to greater satisfaction in many companies. For example, in many companies, the thermostat is set particularly low over the weekend until Monday morning, often making it feel as if the workday starts in a refrigerator. Also, noise pollution can be quickly addressed, for instance, by making large open-office landscapes more modular.

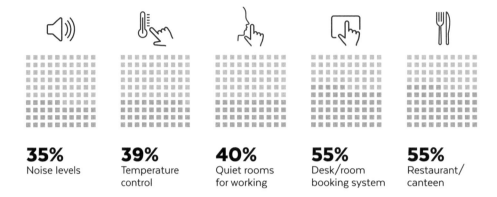

35%	39%	40%	55%	55%
Noise levels	Temperature control	Quiet rooms for working	Desk/room booking system	Restaurant/ canteen

Figure 2.4: Factors affecting employee satisfaction – Leesman: the workplace reset report 2023.

IOT: WHAT DO YOUR DEVICES TELL YOU?

Later in this book, we discuss extensively how technology contributes to better FM, thanks to the data these technologies provide. Concepts such as 'digital twins' and 'smart buildings' are thoroughly explored. But one form of technology also deserves a spot in this data-focused chapter: the Internet of Things, or IoT. The Internet of Things essentially involves adding intelligence to all devices and connecting them to central systems so they can share information remotely and independently monitor and control certain aspects. For buildings, this means, among other things, that HVAC, lighting, security, and energy management can be locally monitored and adjusted as needed, and the occupancy rate can be closely followed. By storing these data centrally and integrating them with each other, you gain insights that, in turn, lead to improved efficiency, comfort, and well-being for building users.

For over ten years, IoT has occupied a place in the hearts and systems of companies. The question is no longer whether to use IoT, but where, when, and why. In other words: where do data generated by IoT add real value, and where is their utility more limited? Targeted deployment and combination of IoT data can lead to useful insights. For instance, discovering that the temperature in certain areas remains too high for extended periods allows us to schedule an intervention, or – if possible – automatically send a signal to the Building Management System to adjust the temperature. But at the same time, you need to consider the cost of IoT, which can be higher than you think, based on this information. It's not just the cost of hardware and software; you also need to invest in many other things: implementation, management, maintenance, training, security, and future-proofing the infrastructure. All these factors must be considered when deciding whether or not to implement an IoT environment.

Fortunately, there are solutions where IoT is offered 'as a service'. This means that the solution provider leases the necessary hardware and software and takes care of management and maintenance, among other things. But even then, the investment in IoT may still seem too high when weighed against the expected return. Every device can tell you something if you invest enough in it, but the story has to be interesting enough.

HOW DO YOU PROCEED?

If you want to develop an effective data strategy, you should keep a few basic rules in mind. First and foremost, you should look at what is already in place. Which systems are you already running, what data do they generate, and what can you do with that data? This consideration should not only include thermostats and other control systems but also badges and access control systems, for example. It's not always easy to get a clear view of this. In many companies, the ICT infrastructure, and thus the associated data, is a real 'spaghetti structure': a disorganised, tangled mess of systems and data. So, the challenge is to bring order to this and turn the spaghetti into a lasagna, with many, orderly layers, where everything can be found quickly.

Next, you need to think about how you want to process the data. What do you want to do manually, automate, and digitalise? How do you ensure that the data go through the various steps: from data to information to insights to wise decisions and interventions? Analysing data is one thing, but basing your decisions on it is even better.

In the future, we will increasingly be able to make smart adjustments in our FM services through diverse forms of AI and algorithms in an integrated environment, leading to greater satisfaction in (and outside of) the workplace. For instance, by combining data on the weather with your own data on registered visitors and workplace occupancy rates, you can make reliable predictions about how many people the cleaning crew will need to deploy. And these choices are then linked to the results contract established between the organisation and the service provider. All data, both internal and external, are actually part of one large data platform: that is the starting point for your data strategy, both today and in the future. Although it may take a long time for many to reach that level of integration, this direction should always be kept in mind.

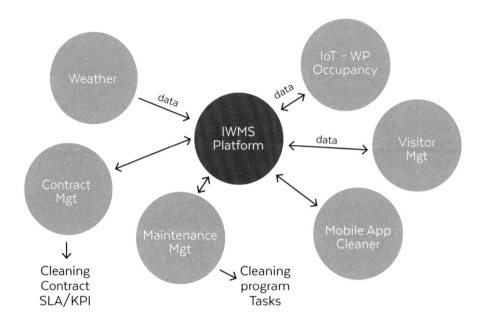

Figure 2.5: An example of data flow integration.

Data management is becoming an integral part of FM. It's crucial to be fully aware of this and draw the necessary conclusions. Hence, IT and other stakeholders should always be involved in both large and small projects and strategic plans. Regardless of whether cloud-based or not, the importance of data security and other fundamental questions about data usage will increasingly need to be considered in all FM decisions.

DIFFERENT DATA FOR DIFFERENT ROLES

FM is a broad field, as has become clear by now. Depending on your role within the FM story, certain data will be very useful for your specific applications, while others might not be relevant at all. Below, we explore the diverse roles and the types of data that can be utilised for each role.

Let's start with **building owners** who offer real estate, including building management. In the competition for the favour of companies, their potential tenants, all weapons are welcome. One of these weapons can be a sustainability certification from WELL, BREEAM, LEED, or another body. Given the focus on sustainability across all companies, such certification naturally leads to a higher ranking on companies' shortlists. Data from the 'Building Management System' can also play a crucial role. Building owners can use the captured data for better management and maintenance. For example, if the performance of HVAC systems starts to decline, they can plan preventive maintenance to avoid failure. They can also make certain data available to the tenant, allowing them to better cater to the well-being and comfort of employees, with optimal settings for sun shading and HVAC based on information about sunlight and outdoor temperature.

Companies/tenants using the buildings can also make use of the aforementioned data, but there are other types of data that interest them. Operational data, teaching them how to manage the building more efficiently and what can be automated. But the so-called CWIS data (Complaints, Wishes, Information, Service Disruption) captured from an IWMS (Integrated Workplace Management System) can also be very useful, for instance, when setting up Service Level Agreements (SLAs) and Key Performance Indicators (KPIs). Setting your FM objectives without this valuable information from employees themselves would be a real waste.

There are also other data that companies can use to gain insights into employee satisfaction and the 'employee journey'. Information about queues in the restaurant, for example, can influence decisions about the selection of catering offered. Or they can use data as an HR and marketing tool. For instance, if the building has solar panels, you might decide to share the data about the energy generated with employees and visitors on a welcome screen at the reception. This way, employees and visitors see the concrete results of the company's efforts, reflecting positively on the organisation's image as a sustainable partner and employer. You can also share other data, such as the status of facility requests. For years, there have been apps that give employees constant access to all this information.

Providers of FM services can utilise data from various sources. Suppliers of soft FM services often focus on occupancy data to schedule services that consider both the cleaners' and building users' needs efficiently. Hard FM providers derive their data mainly from Building Management Systems (BMS), with a particular focus on occupancy to determine where and when to focus on delivering comfort through their services. Companies offering Integrated Facility Management (IFM) services pay equal attention to both data types, as they play roles at both the infrastructure level and in ensuring well-being.

Real estate developers are also keen on specific types of data, particularly those that provide insights into what is needed to construct future-oriented work environments. This data helps determine the technology integrated into new or renovated buildings. They are already capturing data on sustainability and occupancy rates and ensuring compatibility with commonly used BMSs. This approach enables potential tenants or owners to use data-driven strategies for FM and workspace planning, marking a significant shift from the past practice of building as quickly and cheaply as possible.

Leesman: the home environment offers employees a better work environment

Elsewhere in this chapter, the importance of data on how well the work environment supports the user is discussed to complete the picture of FM. While it's possible to have a good grasp of the ratio between teleworking and office work, as well as the temperature in every room without understanding how well the work environment supports the user's tasks and how the employee feels about their work environment, it remains unclear if and how this contributes to greater employee satisfaction and well-being, which is one of the key goals for every Facility Manager.

Fortunately, organisations like Leesman objectively seek out this satisfaction and the factors contributing to it. The Leesman methodology has been around for 13 years and has gathered responses from over a million respondents. Using this vast data pool, Leesman conducts research to identify trends or find statistical correlations, aiding organisations in creating better workplaces for their employees. For instance, Ericsson used Leesman data on employee interaction with their workplace and work activities to develop five employee personas, providing insights into future office needs. These personas served as the basis for workspace planning, influencing everything from the design of meeting rooms to desk allocation.

Another example is the Government Property Agency (GPA) in the UK, which works on enhancing the workplace reputation in the public sector. This organisation exemplifies that providing an excellent work environment is not solely the prerogative of the private sector. It's not about how much is spent; it's about understanding the needs of hybrid users well. GPA uses Leesman insights to make evidence-based decisions for their employees, aiming for better and creating a workplace that goes beyond the building to understanding the people using the space.

And the results of some surveys immediately provoke thought. "Only 4 out of the 21 (according to Leesman) standard work activities are better supported in the average office than at home," says Pierrick Masure, Development Director at Leesman. "From this, you can deduce two things. One: the effectiveness of most workplaces is at best mediocre. And an average workplace experience is no longer good enough today and in the future! Two: most employees have many reasons to prefer working from home."

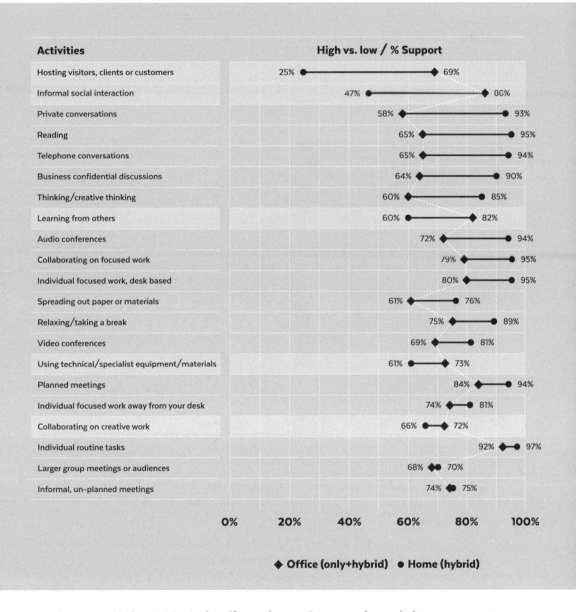

Figure 2.6: Work activities in the office vs. home – Leesman: the workplace reset report 2023.

Among the few activities that employees feel are better supported in the office, we find: receiving visitors and clients, informal social interaction, and learning from each other. Among the better performers – companies that have achieved a Leesman+ certification – we see other activities better supported in the office, including: relaxing and taking breaks together, using technical and specialised equipment, creative collaborations, informal meetings, and meetings with a larger audience. Pierrick summarises as follows: "Individual focus activities and (confidential) conversations are generally better supported at home. Meetings and collaborative activities are supported about equally well at home and in the office. Encounters are generally better facilitated in the office."

THE OFFICE AS A HOTEL?

Pierrick Masure

According to Pierrick Masure, the preference of employees for the home office, besides the fact that the home work environment offers better support for many activities, also has to do with so-called 'hotelification': "Many think this means the office should look like a hotel lobby, with lots of luxury, soft seating, and so forth. But actually, the term refers to something entirely different. As employees no longer commute to the office daily, this workplace is no longer a given. Their perception has changed, making them much more critical of the facilities. Previously, they paid less attention because there was a kind of 'automaticity': going to the office was just part of the job. That's no longer the case. Then you quickly get the question: 'Do they have my choice of 'plant-based' milk that I use at home?'. Where previously the cost of going to the office was seen as a standard monthly expense included in the household budget, today it is associated with a 'cost to go to work'. Working from home is then equated with: no transport, no lunch, no snack, no traffic jams, more me-time etc. The office must then ensure it is worth the total cost of the commute. If the employee also experiences it this way, they will decide to go to the office more often."

Data can play a significant role in FM, whether you're an owner, tenant, service provider, or investor. The specific data you need might depend on your role within FM, but the underlying motivation and process remain consistent. Properly leveraging data not only allows for further, more targeted digitalisation and automation but also provides enriching insights that lead to improved business strategies and operations, ultimately increasing employee satisfaction.

To effectively utilise data, it's advisable to follow these steps:
1. Assess your current position and IT landscape.
2. Define your objectives, deliverables and output.
3. Determine what to digitalise or handle manually. What technology do you need?
4. Establish a project team (stakeholders).
5. Integrate data usage into your core FM strategy.
6. Reflect on how you perceive hotelification.
7. Implement a dashboard for viewing and combining all relevant data.

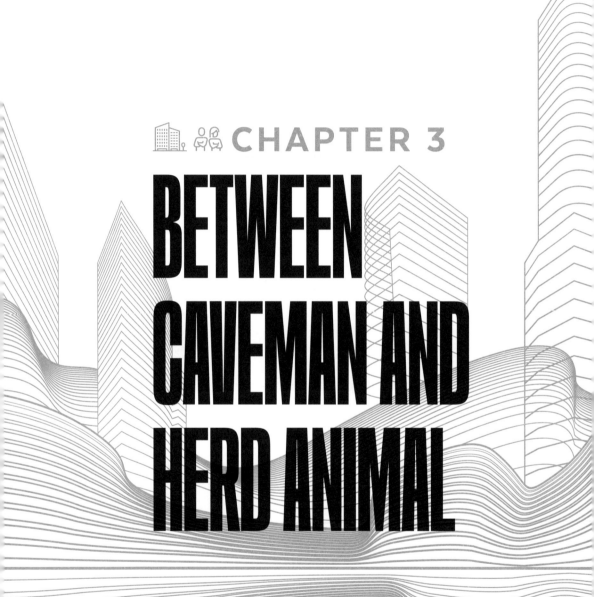

CHAPTER 3

BETWEEN CAVEMAN AND HERD ANIMAL

D o you recall how you worked 20 years ago? For me, it feels like an eternity has passed, but I remember it vividly. Every day, I arrived at the office around 8 a.m. – nice and early, to clear all my administrative and planning tasks before all the other colleagues trickled in. Everyone had their fixed spot, which was taken for granted back then. And each one had their own desktop and telephone set; that was also the rule. We even sent our contracts to clients via fax. It feels like office prehistory, yet this was the typical office environment 20 to 25 years ago.

I was allowed to work from home back then, but honestly, there wasn't much you could do. Taking paperwork home, communicating via email and Skype for video calls – that was pretty much it. Thankfully, laptops, Blackberrys, and other mobile devices gradually found their way to office workers, keeping us digitally connected, even at home and on the move. Working anytime and anywhere increasingly became a reality. But as the boundary between work and private life began to blur, the concept of 'work-life balance' gained importance.

And then came the pandemic, and everything changed.

In this chapter, we delve into the evolution of humans in the workplace and hybrid working. We explore how offices can adapt to these changing needs and how we transition from macro to micro planning. We also review the characteristics of a future-proof work environment. Other important facets discussed include building communities, inclusion and neurodiversity in the workplace, and the role of the Workplace Experience Manager in this story.

COVID CHANGED EVERYTHING

Back to 2020. Specifically, March 2020, when a virus from the East swept over us and would forever change our private and professional lives. Our workplace, in all possible senses, would never be the same again. Previously, it was very simple: our workplace was the building we went to day in and day out to perform our labour. Neither the location nor its arrangement was ever deeply questioned. "Working 9 to 5" (as Dolly Parton sang in the movie of the same name) was the norm, and deviations were few. In the first decades of this century, we saw timid attempts by companies to break this status quo and enable home and remote working, but in at least as many organisations, resistance from management and employees was very high.

But then the pandemic swept through our world, and 'boom', overnight, the worker was transformed from a social being and herd animal into a modern version of the caveman. Companies rapidly switched from office to home working, and FM, human resources (HR), and IT departments had to join forces to make this home working feasible. Initially, this led to primitive conditions for many employees. The kitchen table was renamed the desk, children – who also had to stay home – continuously interrupted the makeshift office, and it turned out that kitchen chairs had not really been designed for sitting on eight hours a day.

Gradually, most companies got to grips with this new situation and ensured their employees had the right resources at home to continue their work in a quality manner: a docking station, a second monitor, an ergonomic office chair, company contribution to the internet connection, etc.

When the pandemic gradually subsided, most of us were thoroughly fed up with the caveman existence and were eager to resume a social work life. We missed the contact and proximity of colleagues and wanted to return to the office to work together and meet again at the coffee machine. Isn't that the place par excellence where you hear the most information, about the company but also about the hobbies and children of your colleagues?

But we can never turn back the clock to the situation before 2020. The fixed workplace and 9-to-5 culture have given way to a company culture that revolves around employee well-being. 'Employee journey' and 'employee experience' are now integral to corporate strategies, and every organisation is looking at how best to fulfil these concepts. Let's briefly explain these two concepts. Employee journey can be viewed from two perspectives. From an HR perspective, it is the journey you take as an employee from the time you join until you leave. From an FM perspective, it's about planning your workday and physically moving from morning to evening through the office/home office/satellite office/etc.

Employee experience refers to the experience you have as an employee while undergoing your employee journey. These concepts are typically also linked to corporate culture, continuous learning, and the different generations active in the workplace. The workplace may be better tailored to everyone's needs, but this has brought a considerable dose of complexity and countless new challenges. The caveman may have traded his warm, cosy, safe workplace for a more social, connected, and varied life, but expectations around that social meeting place are high. And the caveman in us still occasionally seeks the peace and comfort of our own cave.

AWAY WITH 'HYBRID WORKING'?

When companies first started alternating between home and office work, it was called 'New Ways of Working' or simply NWOW. After the pandemic, the term 'hybrid working' emerged. As far as I'm concerned, they can suppress this term again. Done with trendy or other labels for what we do today – working where and when it suits everyone best – we now simply call this 'working', no more. At least that's how I see it, but it will take a while before the whole market is convinced. Therefore, in this book, we will continue to use 'hybrid working' as a term.

I personally made that transition a long time ago. Long before we were forced to work from home, I already worked everywhere: in the office, at home, with clients, in meeting rooms etc. always with the necessary tools to perform my work optimally. And I was far from the only one. But we were still vastly in the minority. Today, this is increasingly being extended to all companies and all employees, so there will no longer be a need for a separate term for it. In the new work reality, companies adopt a labour philosophy and practice focused on providing more flexibility and autonomy to employees, among other things by making better use of available technology. The objective is twofold: on the one hand, to improve work performance, and on the other, to increase employee satisfaction.

This includes both working hours and workplaces being flexible: no 9-to-5 as the only schedule, but also no fixed spot in the office as before. Technology makes remote collaboration almost as efficient as being in each other's vicinity. Employees are no longer judged on their presence but on the results of their work (which requires a significant adjustment in management style for many managers). Autonomy and the associated responsibility for one's own work become the new guiding principles, and the control culture of the past gives way to a culture of trust between employer and employee.

Work is no longer bound by place and time. In addition to home and office work, there are various alternatives: satellite offices, working on the go, co-working spaces, and even working abroad (sometimes referred to as 'Digital Nomads').

All options exist, although some are more successful than others. For example, the demand for satellite offices or co-working spaces where you sit with employees from other companies is rather limited; those who go to an office often do so mainly to see their own colleagues 'live' again and to catch up. Many providers of such co-working spaces are therefore in bad shape today. However, companies are increasingly interested in a shared building, where other companies have their (head) offices; this often promotes interesting interaction and possibly even new business opportunities. And more importantly, shared facilities that are offered by the building manager/owner can be shared by tenants. This could include a gym, a trendy sandwich bar, a coffee bar, a grocery store, and so on.

A NEW APPROACH IS REQUIRED

With all these changes in work habits, different locations, and all other adjustments that the new working conditions entail, it's advisable to thoroughly review and adjust the company policy to fit this new world of work. This policy must comply with local laws and regulations but also, and more importantly, with the new ways of working. Specifically, this policy should be based on Activity-Based Working (ABW), where employees have the freedom to choose different workspaces based on the nature of their tasks. Instead of a fixed desk, they have access to various types of workspaces, such as quiet rooms, meeting rooms, open workspaces, and also the home office. You could also call it 'Event-based Working' (EBW), where the emphasis is more on choosing a workspace based on the day's events: meetings, work lunches, brainstorming sessions... The difference between EBW and ABW is rather small, but 'event-based' emphasises the new reality: people come to the office mainly to engage in activities with colleagues, and this should be taken into account when arranging the company building.

CHANGE MANAGEMENT DESERVES FULL ATTENTION

When developing and implementing a new workplace concept, the importance of change management can hardly be overstated. You will notice this yourself if you read through the various concrete testimonials throughout this book. The success of such a change depends not only on the physical infrastructure and technological facilities but also on how effectively the organisation deals with the changes. Everything impacted by workplace changes – processes, culture, employee behaviour... – deserves due attention. Change management is a holistic approach that addresses the human side of changes in organisations. By applying carefully tailored strategies, change management helps create acceptance, engagement, and successful implementation of new workplace concepts. The extent of change management needed can vary greatly from one company to another. In the diagram below, for example, you notice how change management depends on the maturity and collaboration culture of the company.

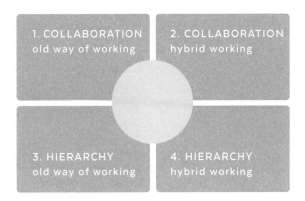

Figure 3.1: Collaboration culture & change.

Companies in the third quadrant need the most change management but can also gain the most benefit from it. Companies in the fourth quadrant mainly need change management focused on leadership and result monitoring. In the first quadrant, change management is mainly about guiding towards the new way of working: here, it's important to get everyone on board with the story. Companies in the second quadrant have already undergone most of the change, and change management will likely be limited to optimisations.

For a successful change management journey, many facets must be addressed. You need to ensure sufficient engagement and communication, both from the company and employees; to regularly check whether everyone is on board and willing to follow through; and to make necessary adjustments based on this feedback. If the willingness to change is not immediately present, extra attention is needed. Adequate time and budget must also be allocated for the training and development of employees. And importantly, show that management fully supports the changes and is actively willing to contribute. Change management is not a one-time exercise. The outcome of this journey should be a sustainable change in behaviour that does not gradually fade, resulting in a reversion to old habits. Therefore, repetition is also very important in communication. At the end of the journey, ideally, there is not just a change in behavior but also a complete cultural shift, where this new way of working is harmoniously integrated.

USE CASE
ESA: CHANGE MANAGEMENT IN PRACTICE

- 12,000m2, (6,000m2 for the workplace) 300 workplaces
- Project timeline: 13 June 2018 - 11 April 2023

Luckily I didn't have to look far for a striking example of the importance of change management. I've been interested in space and science fiction stories since I was a child. So when I heard about the change management story at the European Space Agency (ESA), I didn't hesitate to contact them. And it turned out to be more than worth it!

Laurent Jauniaux, Head of HQ Real Estate & Facilities Management at ESA Headquarters, told me how, just before Covid, they already had in mind a complete redesign of the workplace into a modern work environment concept. The onset of the pandemic made everyone more receptive to change. Yet, the organisation invested a great deal of time and budget in the change management journey that ran parallel to the workplace change: "We used a change management consultant. They conducted an extensive series of workshops, attended by about a third of our community. The workshops consisted of five sessions, each of which was also shared with everyone afterward. The first session compared the old and new models so one could see what would really change. The next session showed

Laurent Jauniaux

comparable workplaces, like PWC in Paris, to demonstrate how it would be and what benefits were achieved. The third session discussed who collaborates with whom and its impact on the workplace layout. In the fourth session, our employees could share their preferences for (or aversions to) possible furniture and other facilities with us. The last session presented a first proposal for a possible model and discussed it. The feedback was processed, and the new proposal went to management.

Notably, the model ultimately implemented barely differed from the first proposal."

ESA also allowed each team the freedom and responsibility to design their own zone. Laurent adds: "They could choose their own furniture from a select catalogue. This sometimes led to remarkable choices. For instance, the FM Team chose six chairs around a table with a tree in the middle. Besides the workshops, the board of directors also gave a speech to the entire organisation each semester to explain the progress, choices, and workshops. And there was constant interaction between the project's steering group and the various teams. All in all, this created a great willingness and even enthusiasm among the employees to move to the new building", notes Laurent: "A survey was recently conducted to gauge the satisfaction and well-being of our employees in the new building, but they didn't wait for it to share their enthusiasm. No one wants to go back to the old way of working, and coming to the office is no longer an obligation like before but a conscious choice for this pleasant work environment."

NEURODIVERSITY AND DESIGN: CREATING A WORKPLACE FOR EVERYONE

Did you know that an estimated 15 to 20% of the population is neurodivergent?[*] Neurodiversity refers to a broad spectrum of neurological characteristics and brain functions in individuals. This includes autism, ADHD, dyslexia, and other neuro-diverse traits. In the past, these individuals were often described as 'suffering from a disorder'. However, there is a growing realisation that this is not a disorder or deviation, but a form of human diversity, just like gender and ethnicity. And that we should aim for a good representation of this category because it only benefits the diversity and resilience of the organisation. According to the creators of the term 'neurodiversity', there is no such thing as a 'standard brain', and everyone varies to a greater or lesser extent from that imaginary standard. For neurodivergent individuals, this variation is just more significant and sometimes more noticeable.

Neurodivergent people are not sick, as is often thought. They simply think, learn, and work differently than neurotypical people. And if they indeed make up a significant percentage of the organisation, you have no choice but to take them into account when designing the ideal workplace. How can you address this? In general, it involves the following principles: ensure a sense of 'belonging and acceptance' by making the work environment as accessible as possible for everyone; adapt your services to this diversity; provide sufficient variety and flexibility in the types of workplaces, so everyone can choose the environment that suits them best; and focus on well-being by monitoring air quality, access to daylight, and natural elements such as wood and plants.

Specifically, look for potentially disturbing factors for neurodivergent individuals and try to neutralise them: noise (too much noise), light (too dark or too bright), temperature (too cold or too warm), too many people or too close together, open or closed spaces etc. Since there are different forms of neurodivergence – you might have hypersensitive individuals on board but also hyposensitive ones – it is important to offer a variety of different types of workplaces, so everyone can make the choice that is right for them. Thus, your workplace becomes an environment with the right balance between focus spaces where one can concentrate well, communal spaces, creative spaces, meeting spaces (for meetings and/or training), recharging spaces or quiet rooms, social spaces, and so on. With due attention to 'living' ('biophilic') elements such as wood and plants and the right colour choice for each room, you can go a long way.

---

* World Economic Forum – How to create a workplace that supports neurodiversity
Inclusion: Why supporting neurodiversity at work matters | World Economic Forum (weforum.org)

UCAS

- 144 workplaces
- Project timeline: Preparation started in 2021 – project finished in 2023

An excellent example of considering neurodiversity as part of a broader effort towards inclusion can be found in the United Kingdom at **UCAS** (the Universities and Colleges Admissions Service, a government service for university and college admissions).

Ian Humphray

Ian Humphray, Workplace Experience Program Manager at UCAS, explained that in designing a new workplace tailored to flexible working, they involved the organisation's diversity teams right from the start. "An internal diversity audit was conducted to map out the needs as accurately as possible."

This focus on diversity resulted in a work environment that is highly accessible and pleasant for individuals with physical disabilities as well as for neurodivergent persons. For instance, there are braille signages at various locations, large pictograms for directions, and height-adjustable desks. Accessibility is a key concern, ensuring it is available to everyone (wheelchairs, crutches, etc.). Electric doors should automatically open upon badge identification. Major spaces must be easily accessible. "Quiet areas and a reading corner with a fireplace, abundant wood and plants within the building, and the option to work or relax in the garden were also incorporated. Blankets are even available for team meetings in the garden. This new workplace thus offers an environment where everyone can thrive," Ian adds. This leads to employee satisfaction exceeding 90% for this new workplace.

So, how do we begin to develop a new workplace concept? Certainly not by haphazardly dropping some furniture onto a blank sheet. It's a complex exercise that requires significant preparation before making any decisions. It starts with thoughtful analyses focusing primarily on your organisation and your employees, as the workplace is ultimately designed for them. You always begin by assembling your project team, ambassadors (stakeholders), and focus groups (specific themes) from various departments. This team is responsible for analysing the company's and employees' needs and, based on that, defining the objectives. They must ensure the company's values are translated into a plan, thereby creating added value. In the analysis phase preceding the macro- and micro-planning, several crucial steps occur: interviews with all parties involved, activity measurements, headcount per department, and the creation of an activity model and a relationship diagram, as shown below, which helps determine which departments should be located near each other. Based on the collected information, employee profiling occurs, and the activities that fit this profile are determined.

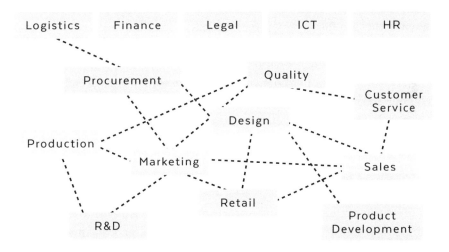

Figure 3.2: Activity overview vs. departments.

Based on the preceding information, you can start developing the concept. It begins with defining the building blocks: What types of workspaces do you need?

Figure 3.3: Various workspace types.

Designing the office workspaces occurs on two levels. At the macro-planning level, you establish the broad layout principles, using a so-called 'stacking and blocking diagram' that determines the different types of workspaces and allows for these blocks to be moved around in the available spaces until everything fits perfectly. Typically, the blocks are also colour-coded according to the organisation. In macro-planning, you also work on zoning, optimising circulation within the workplace. You create so-called 'neighbourhoods', areas tailored to specific activities. For instance, an HR neighbourhood can be designed with a portion of shared workspaces but also necessary small meeting spaces to discuss confidential matters, creating the ideal mix with tasks that need to be done and that are inherent to the 'profiles' in your organisation.

Micro-planning, on the other hand, is a more detailed study, where you might, for example, create a layout per floor, and determine which types of walls, furniture, and other necessities will be used. Nowadays, these are often choices for sustainable materials, as part of the overall strategy around environmentally conscious and sustainable business practices. This strategy also indirectly ensures the choice of modular systems. This way, you can easily reuse existing building blocks in a workspace reorganisation instead of having to purchase/set up a whole new workspace.

After these phases, we move on to procurement, executing the layout, moving employees to the new workspace, and evaluation and aftercare. These steps aren't surprising for anyone familiar with project management. My tips for the entire workplace trajectory might sound familiar, but I'd still like to share them. Ensure it's a journey where you maintain high engagement by communicating sufficiently in both directions. Form a team with ambassadors from different departments. Organise 'town halls' (large-scale information sessions). Set up test arrangements and organise workshops.

A WORKSPACE MAKEOVER

Since an image speaks louder than a thousand words, I'd like to illustrate the impact of the activity-based - and event-based - method on office layout with a vivid example. A small disclaimer here: I deliberately kept the images as colourless and abstract as possible to not distract from the concept and layout. An ideal workspace can certainly be very colourful, but in these sketches, it would only have been distracting.

We start with a typical office layout according to the old way of working.

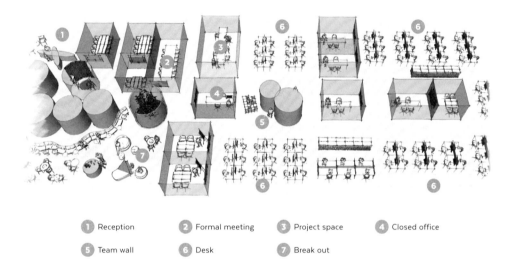

1 Reception   2 Formal meeting   3 Project space   4 Closed office

5 Team wall   6 Desk   7 Break out

Figure 3.4: Office environment: old way of working.

Here, we see a traditional office setup. Flexible workspaces may have already made their entrance, but we still observe a plethora of closed offices, traditional meeting rooms, etc. It's more of a one-size-fits-all and is not really inviting for the employee to spend time here.

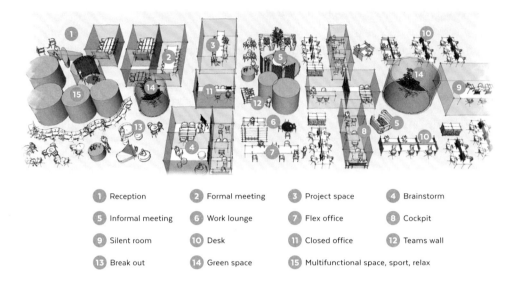

1 Reception	**2** Formal meeting	**3** Project space	**4** Brainstorm
5 Informal meeting	**6** Work lounge	**7** Flex office	**8** Cockpit
9 Silent room	**10** Desk	**11** Closed office	**12** Teams wall
13 Break out	**14** Green space	**15** Multifunctional space, sport, relax	

Figure 3.5: Hybrid working office environment.

In the new workplace concept, we see a shift in workspace types; there's much more diversity, and the focus on tasks, events, and activities has taken precedence. The layout is tailored to collaboration and gathering. Individual offices or assigned workspaces have completely disappeared here.

THE WORKPLACE AS A REFLECTION OF YOUR BUSINESS STRATEGY

Is the second drawing above then the model par excellence for every company that wants to embrace the new way of working? Absolutely not. As I've already mentioned, each company must start with its analysis, take its values, standards, and core values, and translate these into its workplace strategy and design. The office can serve as an anchor point in the company culture. And just as every company culture is somewhat unique, this can also be the case for office layout.

It is, therefore, extremely important to give this adequate thought. What does your company stand for? How can you bring your values to the forefront? If your workplace also radiates these values, you turn your work environment into a powerful signal, both to your own employees and to the outside world and potential new talent. You can use the well-known 'balanced scorecard' (Kaplan and Norton) to measure and improve the company's performance in **four areas**: financial, employee relationship, internal process, and innovation and growth. Once you have gained insight into the strengths, weaknesses, and values of the organisation, you can then design the workplace in such a way that it supports your business strategy.

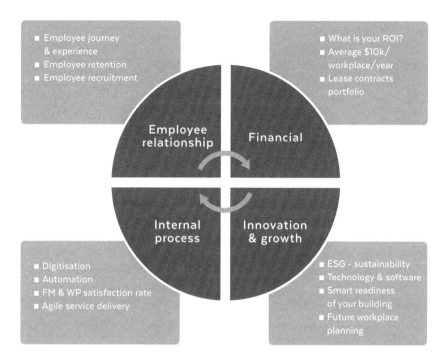

Figure 3.6: Balanced scorecard for your workplace environment.

ACCENTURE PORTUGAL

- 3,400 m², 225 workstations
- Project timeline: start January 2020 – end February 2023

A company that has succeeded wonderfully in this endeavour is Accenture Portugal. Sara De Oliveira, their Workplace Business Operations Senior Manager, explains their project: "We wanted to bring together the different floors of the former headquarters into one building that is fully equipped for the work of tomorrow, with an eye to remote working, flexible onsite working, but also for diverse work needs.

Sara De Oliveira

We wanted to be recognised as typically Accenture but also as a Portuguese company. That's why we incorporated discrete cultural references to Lisbon in the design. We translated our value of inclusion into maximum accessibility and facilities so that it is accessible to everyone. Our focus on sustainability is found not only in the construction principles themselves and our sensors and measuring systems but also in the choice of materials, with a preference for local and natural materials and products. And as a technologically advanced company, we have of course also provided plenty of technology, but mainly for better and seamless work experiences and to keep everyone connected, in all senses of the word."

1. FM vs Workplace Experience

With the current focus on Workplace Experience (WEX), many get the impression that FM no longer has a role to play in current business operations. Is this true? Is the role of the Facility Manager coming to an end? And will we soon see only workplace experience managers? In my opinion, it won't come to that. I see both functions as complementary rather than mutually exclusive. The Facility Manager concerns themselves with broader aspects than just the 'workplace': the buildings and furnishings, the spaces and how to maintain and manage them, the technology and data, the real estate aspects, and other concrete issues like sustainability and reusability.

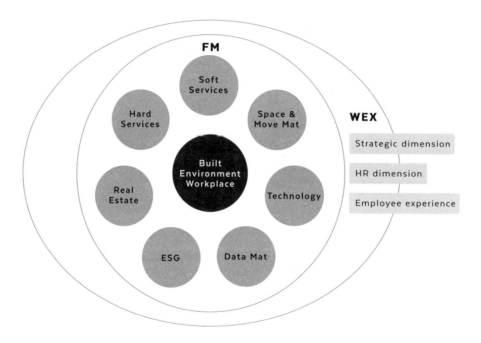

Figure 3.7: FM & Workplace Experience Manager.

In Workplace Experience, these topics are also covered. However, an additional dimension is added: the strategic and Human Resources dimension. The workplace experience manager not only looks at all those material aspects but also considers how they can contribute to the employee's experience at the workplace. Thus, the WEX manager can contribute to various strategic objectives of the organisation: employee branding, recruitment and retention, company culture, and stakeholder management (including financial and IT stakeholders, as well as employees and external parties). In my view, FM and Workplace Experience Management are not an either/or but a both/and story: both functions have their place within the organisation, but each focuses on different aspects.

2. Real Estate dilemmas

With the breakthrough of flexible working, where office work and home work regularly alternate, office spaces are, of course, much less utilised than before. When offices are redesigned to improve the workplace experience, this usually also involves a significant reduction in office space. After all, no one needs unused office space, especially given its cost. In the Benelux, for example, an average workspace for 1 FTE (Full Time Equivalent) costs between 10,000 and 12,500 euros per year.[*] The cost can vary significantly depending on several factors. Location plays a major role; a prime location in the city centre naturally costs more than a building somewhere in the countryside. But the amenities and services the company offers to its employees also determine the cost of a workspace. Then there are factors such as the type of workspace (traditional or co-working workspace, flexible buildings etc.), the company size (number of employees), and the costs for location amenities (prime city centre location or location near a train station) and employee mobility.

Therefore, we can expect an avalanche of commercial office spaces. However, this might be less extreme than initially expected. It was thought that an average of 40 to 50% of square metres would be shed. Now, we see that this is more likely to be between 20 and 30%. Notably, the reduction of satellite offices in favour of centralisation is prominent.

When deciding to dispose of or retain real estate, careful consideration is required, with a thorough analysis of the pros and cons of each choice. The choice of constructing a new building or renovating an existing one is also part of this analysis. And if a move is chosen, the location of the new building plays a crucial role. Where do most employees come from, and what is the distance to the office? Where does the company want to recruit? Are there many schools and universities nearby? And what is the weight of the location, considering the percentage of work time still spent in the office? In short: even the choice of office building for the future involves more consideration than you might think.

---

[*] Source: Colliers: Occupier Cost Index 2024

3. Modularity

In addition to the individual choice of what is best for the company, when choosing a specific type of office building, one should also consider the immediate surroundings. Everyone is familiar with 'ghost towns', districts full of office buildings that buzz with activity from 8 a.m. to 8 p.m. and then fall silent. This model, where a neighbourhood is only active for half of the time, is far from sustainable, creating a sense of insecurity for those who happen to be there outside these office hours. It's not sustainable urban development, if you ask me.

Increasingly, we should look to neighbourhoods where there is continuous activity, where office buildings are also used for recreation, where offices in the same building coexist with apartments, restaurants, or taverns. In short: an environment where there is always something happening. In the Middle East they are already applying these concepts in several 'Mega projects', eg. NEOM project in the Kingdom of Saudi Arabia. Those who design or redesign a building today should take this into account. Ensure that your building is multi-functional and modular, able to be used for various types of activities. The office building of the future may initially be filled with offices, to be partially converted years later into a mix of offices, apartments, and/or retailers. If we can generate this dynamism, there will naturally be less vacant space, and we can make optimal use of the available square metres, which will inevitably become scarcer.

A future with modular and thus sustainable buildings – who could object to that?

1. Start by establishing a hybrid working policy.
2. Conduct a thorough analysis of your real estate portfolio and base your choices on this (surface area, locations, stay or go...).
3. Develop your design on both a macro and micro level.
4. Provide ample attention to change management.
5. Consider inclusion and neurodiversity.
6. Work sustainably, in terms of materials as well as location choice and other aspects.
7. Get inspired by examples that set the standard.

CHAPTER 4

TECHNOLOGY : THE ESSENTIAL BUILDING BLOCK

Can you overestimate the importance of technology in FM? In my opinion, certainly not. I must admit: I am slightly biased. Twenty years ago, I started my career in the technology sector for FM, specifically at an international IWMS player (MCS – Spacewell). What exactly IWMS means will be explained later in this chapter. After that, I also worked for several major technology players such as Canon, the market leader in digitalisation and document flow optimisation, and Planon, the leader in the IWMS market. But even with other companies, I was always involved in software-related matters, and I have always closely followed the evolution of this market. It is also no complete coincidence that I have taken on the Technology & Innovation Lead function on the board at IFMA Belgium.

Actually, it goes without saying that technology will play an important role in all aspects of FM. But you should always keep in mind that technology must remain a tool, and never become a goal in itself. Always start from your business case and then look at where and why you would use software or other technology. However, to do that, you need to be fully aware of what kind of technology is available. And the range has increased enormously over the past ten years. You just need to compare your own smartphone and the apps that run on it with what you had ten years ago, and you already get an idea of the journey we have taken over the course of that time.

Especially for FM, the advent of 5G and the connectivity we achieve with it mark a spectacular development. Consider, for example, the real-time monitoring of systems in your buildings, which enables prescriptive maintenance, where problems can be quickly identified and resolved, thereby increasing operational reliability. Also, the amount of available data thereby increases exponentially (we discussed this extensively in Chapter 2). And these are just some of the technological evolutions with which we can support and improve FM in all areas.

In this chapter, we will discuss, among other things, IWMS, the de facto standard in terms of software for FM and workplace management, and we will discuss how the IWMS of the future, named CPIP, is already peeking around the corner. You will receive some practical tips for setting up a technology project. And you will learn how a building can benefit from a digital twin. We will continue with testimonies from companies that have successfully implemented technology. And we will end with an ideal vision of where you can go with technology.

WHY IMPLEMENT TECHNOLOGY?

As stated in the introduction, technology is not a goal in itself. It supports solving issues. Before we dive into technology, it seems interesting to me to highlight some of these.

There is a **scarcity in the labour market**, and this is also felt in the FM world. We want to manage the people we have available as efficiently as possible. As a result, we need to optimally deploy our processes and automate where possible.

The **comfort** of building users is central; from an FM perspective, you want to make the employee journey as pleasant as possible. We will briefly map this out at the end of the chapter.

Another assignment is centralising and having the necessary **data** available.

Not just having data, but being able to make decisions for the future and to monitor the quality of the service. Think of it as your '**business intelligence**', your single pane of glass.

Basing FM services on '**real-time**' data so that it can be adjusted to the needs, especially with the occupancy rates in office buildings.

So far, we have answered the 'why question'; in the rest of this chapter, we focus on the 'what question': What kind of technology is available for use, and how can FM take advantage of it?

IWMS: THE ULTIMATE MANAGEMENT SYSTEM FOR FACILITY MANAGERS

As mentioned before: as far as management systems for FM go, IWMS has become the standard. Yet you will often also come across other terms (usually in the form of acronyms), which can lead to confusion. FMIS (Facility Management Information System), CMMS (Computerised Maintenance Management System), CAFM (Computer Aided Facilities Management), EAM (Enterprise Asset Management) etc. It is, in itself, already an impressive list of variants or precursors to the current management systems. But IWMS (Integrated Workplace Management System) truly fulfils the promise of its name: it integrates various aspects of workplace management. This includes tools for 'real estate portfolio management' but also for making a floor plan and so much more. It contains more digital tools for the Facility Manager than any other software. But even here, it's best to keep in mind: IWMS is not a goal in itself. It only offers support for the facility processes, which in turn support the core processes of the company.

WHERE CAN YOU TURN TO?

To get an idea of the IWMS suppliers market, I like to make use of the 'Green Quadrant' from research firm Verdantix, based on extensive research of this market.

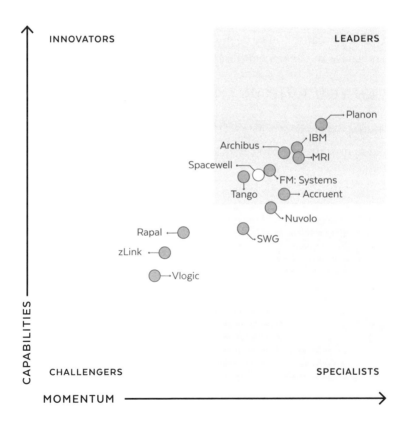

Figure 4.1: Green Quadrant: Integrated Workplace Management Systems 2022 – Verdantix.

A few remarks on this:

1. In the past, you had to purchase this software, and such an investment was considered a capital expenditure (capex). Nowadays, these platforms are mostly offered in an operational expenditure (opex) model, cloud-based Software as a Service (SaaS) that you can rent.

2. Most IWMS systems already include a significant number of functionalities by default. But every company is different, and therefore often looks for custom development. My advice? Start by offering standard solutions, and reduce customisation. This makes it easier and quicker for FM managers to implement things but also to immediately clarify which processes are supported. Custom features can still be developed afterwards, but by then you will have already experienced what the system is able to do and what it can't do. Another piece of advice: If the processes supported by the IWMS do not align with your own processes, you might want to take a moment to critically examine your own processes. Just because you've been doing something one way for many years doesn't mean it can't be done differently and better.

WHAT CAN YOU FIND IN AN IWMS?

An IWMS is typically composed of various modules. This is why it is referred to as a modular approach. Some of the most frequently recurring modules in most IWMSs include:

Figure 4.2: Overview of IWMS modules.

IWMSs provide various stakeholders with support for challenges and answers to specific questions. Previously, the software's aim was to ensure the lifespan of the building and was mainly used for maintenance and everything that entailed. Later, aspects were added to further optimise operational management, such as space management and move planning (indeed, everyone used to have their fixed workplace, and there was a lot of moving around within buildings). Over the last ten years, there has also been more focus on soft services and the comfort of building users. How can you leverage your 'hospitality' factor with your IWMS? Make services easily accessible. And the most recent step we have seen is making data available to improve well-being, not just comfort, in our workplace.

WHO BENEFITS FROM IWMS?

IWMS can serve all the players in the FM arena:

The **building owner** finds support to make the buildings operate as energy-neutral as possible. Often, they will link the IWMS to the BMS (Building Management System) to automate processes. Furthermore, IWMS also assists them in lease contract management and portfolio management, and in striving for compliance with regulations.

The **building users** (the companies) can employ IWMS for optimal 'hospitality' by making services – such as reporting issues with the coffee machine, ordering catering, booking a room, etc. – easily accessible for employees. They can also further invest in hybrid working by providing, among other things, a smooth reservation system.

The **FM service provider** finds in IWMS useful tools for optimising processes, and to link reporting around SLAs and KPIs to 'real-time' data of their services. This includes the evolution of contract forms towards data-driven contracts. Considering the labour market's scarcity, an IWMS optimises these processes and automation, allowing you to be more efficient with your people. Later in this chapter, I will discuss this with ISS and their Group CIDO (CIO / CDO).

The 'real estate developer' is responsible for designing and building the buildings. They do not primarily work within an IWMS but rather focus on building a 'digital twin' based on a BIM (Building Information Modelling), which simply put is a 3D drawing with all the data of the building. The data they can extract from this digital twin are crucial for use in the later exploitation of buildings. Therefore, the digital twins are usually linked to an IWMS to better deploy the data in managing the building.

Whatever your role, IWMSs help you in several crucial areas. The information is centralised, so everyone works with the same truth (this has not always been the case). Processes are automated, leading to more efficient business operations. FM services are more easily accessible. You cater to the comfort of building users. You have more control over the entire FM narrative, thanks to extensive reporting and clear dashboards. And – last but not least – the chance of human error is significantly reduced when everything is digitised and centralised.

'LEVERAGE YOUR "HOSPITALITY FACTOR" WITH YOUR IWMS. MAKE SERVICES EASILY ACCESSIBLE.'

PETER ANKERSTJERNE

Chief Executive Officer (CEO) at Planon.

As CEO at Planon, the market leader in the IWMS software market, Peter Ankerstjerne has a clear view on the use of technology in the FM sector.

"A lot is happening in the world of technology for FM. AI, IoT, and sensor technology contribute to smarter buildings and workplaces. The integration of these technologies into IWMS and other platforms has a significant impact on all stakeholders.

These stakeholders are all willing to invest in technology, but for various reasons, Peter observes: "In recent years, we noticed that companies using the buildings want to be more 'agnostic', thus less dependent on FM service providers managing their data for them. They increasingly want to consult their own data and act flexibly, without relying on their service providers' digital tools. FM service providers, on the other hand, want to use technology as a means to integrate their resource planning and workflow management directly with the end-user, thereby becoming more flexible and efficient, and evolving towards on-demand services and value-based contracts. Building owners also want more control over their data and software solutions, but as a way to innovate, differentiate, and position themselves, for example, as sustainable businesses, and to contribute to the workplace experience their customers are looking for." Yet, the pace at which they invest remains slower than in other sectors, given the small margins in this market, and the often old infrastructure on which they have to implement this new technology.

When companies approach him for advice, he usually gives the same two tips: "First: make use of open standards and platforms. You will only really reap the benefits of your digital environment if it is part of a larger ecosystem. With open platforms that can hook into different ecosystems, you can make a difference. Second: start small. Such an ecosystem can be overwhelming, and then it's good to start with a small project that you can still link to the systems of your partners and suppliers, thanks to that open approach." In the near future, Peter sees AI (Artificial Intelligence) especially playing a major role: "You will be able to utilise your data much better and work much more proactively by anticipating changing employee and user behaviour, anticipating potential problems, and predicting new needs before they actually occur." Furthermore, he sees the FM technology market growing in the coming years, if only because major technology players like Microsoft, Cisco, Schneider Electric, and Siemens have set their sights on the workplace environment.

In conclusion, Peter strongly believes in the importance of technology, not only in terms of efficiency and new insights: "The FM sector is an ageing sector. Many FM specialists will soon retire, and we do not immediately see a next generation replacing them. To attract young talent, we need technology among other things. With the challenging projects that technology makes possible, we can make our sector more attractive to that generation. We are also on the eve of a 'Worktech revolution' where we can achieve enormous productivity gains by focusing on smarter buildings – and the smart technology that makes this possible."

"TECHNOLOGY WILL MAKE FM MORE ATTRACTIVE AND PRODUCTIVE"

Anyone who follows the technology world, whether from a distance or up close, is familiar with this phenomenon: when a platform or system is fully mature and stable, suppliers and analysts decide it's time for something new. This is now also happening with IWMS: just as this software market has fully matured, its designated successor has already emerged. And, just like its predecessor, this technology also has a catchy acronym: CPIP (short for Connected Portfolio Intelligence Platform).

Joy Trinquet

Joy Trinquet, Senior Analyst at research and advisory firm Verdantix, has been following this new platform for some time and is eager to explain why she sees CPIP eventually taking over from IWMS: "Historically, IWMS has been very good at managing FM, but with the advent of cloud and IoT, a new playing field has developed, and the management platforms have to follow suit. This is where CPIP comes in: this platform takes all the connected solutions such as IoT devices or external systems and apps from third parties into account much more. Where IWMS was typically good at portfolio, space, and asset management, but less so in processing and analysing IoT data or connecting with third-party solutions and operational systems, CPIP excels in both. Thanks to the cloud-based approach of CPIPs, management can be made more efficient, faster, and cheaper. In short: a promising successor." With the launch of a new name and products in the market, it doesn't suddenly happen all at once. Joy tempers expectations: "The breakthrough of CPIP will happen gradually. Only in five years do we see this platform becoming fully integrated. But it is important that you know what is coming, so you can start thinking about where you want to be in the long term. Because you can be sure that CPIP will break through sooner or later."

Smart buildings, digital twins... with CPIP, we already got a glimpse into the future. Are we now fully on the path to the future? Not quite; much of what we describe below is already common practice today. But first things first: What exactly are smart buildings and digital twins?

A **'smart building'** can be briefly defined as a sustainable building that, thanks to intelligent design, the necessary installations, and connected systems, can be used and managed efficiently. A smart building offers individual building users optimal comfort and a pleasant user experience, and provides a variety of services to building users, building managers, and external parties.

A **'digital twin'** is an identical digital copy of a construction. This can be a building (group), a bridge, a highway, an urban district, or even an entire city. In the construction sector, a digital twin is also called a data twin or virtual model. In many cases, BIM is also connected to this. But what is this exactly?

BIM stands for Building Information Modelling, an advanced digital approach to designing, constructing, and managing buildings. BIM goes beyond traditional 2D drawings by creating a detailed digital model of a building that contains information about geometry, materials, physical and functional characteristics. After construction, the BIM model becomes a valuable resource for Facility Managers. The model contains information about all the components of the building, including material specifications, locations of technical systems, and maintenance instructions. This facilitates the management of maintenance, repairs, and planning renovations. In short, BIM enables FM professionals to work more accurately and efficiently throughout the entire life cycle of an office building, from design and construction to day-to-day management. It promotes collaboration, improves communication, and optimises processes. It's important to note that not all information in the BIM model is necessary for your FM operations; which data to integrate into an IWMS must be analysed. A clear data protocol needs to be put in place.

Digital twins essentially serve as an anchor for all IoT in the office and smart building systems. All data streamed from sensors and connected devices are collected in this digital twin, which then makes the data available to various workplace software (IWMS), which, in turn, can transform the data into comprehensive insights about the workplace. Thus, digital twins contribute to better decisions based on the right information, and therefore to better workplaces. Chapter 2 provides more information on what IoT can contribute to information.

When different systems are present (BMS, IWMS, IoT), 'openness' is of crucial importance. Open standards are essential for connecting systems and enabling them to communicate. Only then will they optimally contribute to your smart building. In other words, a building only becomes truly smart if it is open to everything happening inside and outside the building. Other tips for working on a smart building? Work 'use case'-driven: with concrete goals in mind, you will achieve results faster and be able to take the next steps. Also, do not make your projects too complex. If the project looms over you like the Himalayas, you will become discouraged from the start, and the chance of success is very small.

A great use case to hang your smart building ambitions on is: How can we promote well-being in our building and make this information available to our colleagues? Sensors in the meeting rooms can measure temperature, CO_2 and humidity. The results can be displayed on a dashboard at the entrance of the respective floor. And you can link them to your IWMS, which generates an automatic alarm and sends a request to contact a technician when certain 'thresholds' are exceeded.

See how you can link your BMS (Building Management System) to your IWMS. The BMS provides the data stream from your technical installations, and you need this data to make your operations 'predictive'. You will notice that in this way, you start creating your 'facility platform' and making your building smarter by using data to perform smarter actions.

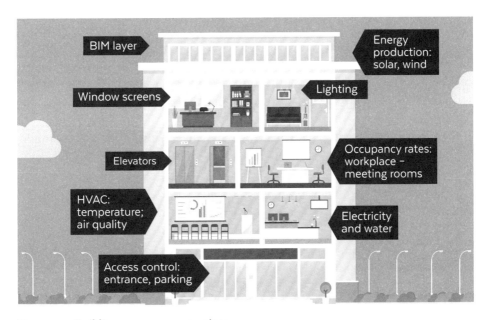

Figure 4.3: Building measurement points.

What data do you then need, and from where will you operate? What are 'avoidable costs'? How can I ensure that we increasingly focus on predictive maintenance? Make sure you focus on user comfort, energy consumption and cost estimation failure. With these parameters coming from the BMS, algorithms and AI can get to work to automate your processes and take your maintenance to the next generation.

The number of sensors is very extensive and there are many types of sensors, as you can see in the diagram above. From temperature and air quality to electricity and water consumption, from elevators to parking lots, from the occupancy rate in meeting rooms and other workspaces to the lighting and curtains – these are all different sources of information that each in their own way can contribute to more well-being in the office.

You can see all this technology as the 'brain' of your building that helps to make your building smarter.

STEPPING INTO THE DIGITAL POOL

It goes without saying that each of us will increasingly employ technology; the digitalisation of our activities and processes is not only inevitable but also very necessary to remain competitive. However, this does not mean that you should jump unprepared and thoughtlessly at every opportunity to digitise. You don't have to dive into the digital world; you can certainly first gauge the temperature and the depth of the water.

What do I specifically mean by this? That you should prepare and consciously take each step towards digitalisation, otherwise you risk achieving lesser results with more digitalisation. Good preparation includes, among other things, the following:

1. The first question you always need to ask is 'why?'. Why do you want to implement this digitalisation? What is your use case? What problem do you want to solve? Provide a clear description of the problem statement and the technological solution that could be used.
2. Take a 'snapshot' of your current organisation and which tools you already have before you list your digitalisation needs for processes. Review this across different departments. Sometimes there are already software packages within the company that can provide certain solutions. If there is no

central IT strategy, be sure to also check with your FM colleagues in other countries/regions.

3. What do you specifically want to achieve as a result of your digitalisation? Is this just for FM or also for management or for HR? What is needed? Taking a close look at the data management model (see figure 2.1) can certainly do no harm here.

4. How do you survey the market for the best solution? Do you choose a targeted solution? Or do you prefer a comprehensive platform? Either way, you must ensure that the project is manageable. If it is too large and complex, divide it into several projects. Work in short sprints to achieve quicker results.

Everything obviously also depends on the size of your company and whether you can make such investments. Budget is a factor that should not be underestimated. Therefore, I also want to mention that there are quite a few 'single point solutions' that can provide a solution for your daily FM. A rule of thumb that you should use: Make sure these systems can integrate with other systems such as an IWMS. This way, you can also continue with these single point solutions in the future. For example, you can think of an IoT sensor just to monitor your meeting room for occupancy rate, temperature, CO_2, etc.

Another tip I can give is integration with systems like Microsoft; for example, integration with Outlook to reserve meeting rooms in your IWMS. These are standard functionalities but double-check with your IT department if you can set this up. A lot has to do with rights and access in your IT environment.

Figure 4.4: The digitalisation train.

ISS: TECHNOLOGY INCREASES VISIBILITY

ISS is by far the largest FM service provider in the world. With their 350,000 employees, they have a global presence in this market. "And because they are all directly employed, ISS can also better monitor the quality of the services delivered," adds Markus Sontheimer, CIDO of ISS Global. ISS also continues to strive for more and better: they want to lead in sustainability and in integrated services. And they also want to be the digital leader in the FM services market. How do you become a digital leader? "Through a clear strategy," Markus replies, "thus we have fully embraced the cloud, but we have also set the highest standard for cybersecurity, to be a full-fledged partner for, among others, banks. We have our own cybersecurity team, and it's necessary. The importance of cybersecurity will only increase with the advent of AI and automation."

As a major player in this market, you also need to become a software integrator yourself, Markus believes: "You need platforms for workplace, for digital twins, so you can analyse and predict customer needs regarding, for example, available space and nutrition. You must seamlessly connect and integrate with the customer environment and also make the tech support seamless. This way, you can play a strategic role for that company."

Markus Sontheimer

Cleaning services seem like very traditional activities that have little to do with innovation and technology. "Yet the opposite is the case with us," Markus counters, "thanks to all our IoT and other data, we can perfectly predict who is where and when, and consequently deploy our people during office hours instead of after. This makes us much more visible but also more appreciated." That's why about 100,000 cleaners are now using a front-end app that tells them how to organise their day. They can also use this app for, among other things, swapping shifts or for leave requests. "Such an app for such a large group is quite a challenging project, but it was worth it. Not only for more efficiency and esteem with the customer, but also because it makes them feel even more involved," Markus notes.

In the near future, Markus also sees a major role for AI at ISS: "For instance, we are now creating a chatbot for that front-end based on AI. This can eliminate language barriers and enable us to promote inclusion for all nationalities." AI and data are powerful tools, but you must handle them correctly, Markus warns: "The customer always remains the owner of their data. He can share it with you, but will not give it away. There are sufficient technologies available to make this sharing happen in the right way. The last thing the customer wants is to feel like they are chained to you for the next ten years. The customer should always feel that they are in a partnership and that there is room for flexibility."

'YOU NEED PLATFORMS FOR WORK-PLACE, FOR DIGITAL TWINS, SO YOU CAN ANALYSE AND PREDICT CUSTOMER NEEDS.'

THE END GOAL: HOW WAS YOUR DIGITAL DAY?

As we have already stated, the 'human' aspect is central to the experience of the workplace environment. As a Facility Manager it is your goal to map out that employee journey well. Let's take a look at such a journey. The end goal of digitalisation is that technology supports you as an employee optimally throughout the day. An app that saves your preferences and makes suggestions based on them should be perfectly possible: Netflix has been succeeding in this for our entertainment for years; why couldn't we do it for the work environment? It can already start at home. I'm already looking forward to a digital assistant that asks me in the morning: "Hi Tom, how are you? Where do you want to work from today?"
I answer: "In Brussels, please."

My digital assistant again: "You choose Brussels. There your preference is for floor 3 WP16. Unfortunately, this is not available now. But I do have a nice alternative nearby: WP21. Shall I reserve it for you?" So my digital assistant can go on for a while: "Do you want a charging station? Do you want a poke bowl for lunch as usual? ..." Wouldn't this give a boost to the workplace experience? You're not yet at the office, but you already feel completely up for it. Of course, the data and privacy aspect is a discussion point, but most employees would probably like to give up some information to get such a service.

7 STEPS TO SUCCESS

1. Ask yourself the question: Why digitalise?
2. Take a snapshot of where you are now. (Technology maturity)
3. What results (deliverables, output) do you want to achieve by deploying technology?
4. How smart is your building?
5. Put the 'Employee journey' at the centre.
6. Map out your FM technology platform strategy for 3 to 5 years.
7. What is available on the market? Single point solution or platform? Survey the market based on well-developed specifications.

CHAPTER 5

WITHOUT COOPERATION, THINGS WILL NOT WORK OUT

Due to the increasing attention from companies on the employee experience, the Facility Manager gains new opportunities. It's a prime chance to elevate FM on the agenda, and to move it to a tactical and even strategic level. Regardless of the focus of your enterprise – whether it's more on HR and the employee, or on finance and cost control, more strategic or process-oriented – you always have the choice to remain with operations or to also make your mark at a tactical and strategic level.

This by no means implies that you should neglect the operational aspect – quite the contrary. But you must be aware that you can and must play a role at all levels. At the operational level, it's important that you continue to ensure service delivery day by day and that you efficiently direct your own teams and FM service providers. On a tactical level, you focus among other things on rolling out the (further) digitalisation of FM and on quality assurance by using reports on achieving the SLAs (Service Level Agreements) and KPIs (Key Performance Indicators). And at a strategic level, for example, you can help determine the workplace strategy and optimise the real estate portfolio for the coming three to five years, and contribute to the development of ESG (Environmental, Sustainability, and Governance) objectives.

The challenge for the Facility Manager remains, of course, to continue excelling at the operational level to show your added value and earn the respect of colleagues, and on the other hand, to demonstrate that you also have an important role to play at other levels. In other words: you want to avoid being seen only as a 'firefighter' and aim to climb the value chain of the organisation. To do this, it is important that you note down all the objectives for yourself at each level – operational, tactical, and strategic – that you can help achieve, and work out how you plan these in the short, medium, and long term. Once you have done this exercise, you are ready to also convince others that you can and must play this role at every level.

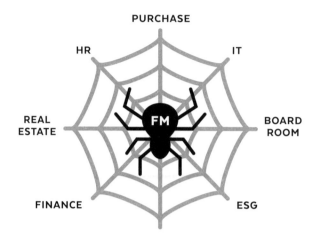

Figure 5.1: FM like a spider in the web.

But how do you get everyone to the point where you can adequately take on your role at all levels? A seat at the table of decision-makers is usually not just granted to you; it must be 'earned'. In practice, this means making yourself indispensable and profiling yourself as an equal business partner to your colleagues in other departments. And you do this best by aligning with them on how your department can contribute to their success.

Not all Facility Managers have mastered this aspect – building bridges between FM and other departments. And I must admit that I have not always been good at this either. I tried to arrange everything from my FM island. But when I realised that I would not get far without the goodwill of other parties, even if I followed all the necessary procedures, I radically changed course and started building those bridges with other departments. That turned out to make a world of difference.

For example, with the HR department, you can align on how the right office concept, tailored to hybrid work, can contribute to their strategy for improving the work experience. With IT, you can actively collaborate on integrating building management systems and IoT into the ICT infrastructure. With the finance department, you can review how the MYMP (multi-year maintenance plan) can be included in the budgets and investments. And with external FM service providers, you can sit down to optimise the service based on needs on the one hand and budgets on the other, and how data can play a role in this. This way, you build a strong bond with all involved players, and you become, as it were, a spider with its own web of connections that you can fall back on to realise your own plans. A spider with eight legs is also a fitting image of the many activities under the purview of the Facility Manager.

KNOW-LIKE-TRUST: THE STEP-BY-STEP PLAN TOWARDS BETTER COLLABORATION

The approach to turning all involved parties into allies closely aligns with the 'know-like-trust' concept used in marketing to foster customer loyalty. This concept is founded on the idea that people are more inclined to buy from a brand with which they have a relationship of trust, and it describes how to develop such a relationship. First, people get to know your brand, then they begin to like it, and eventually, they learn to trust your brand. I became familiar with this concept from my experience in sales and marketing. It quickly became clear to me that this concept was also perfectly applicable in FM, to the journey a Facility Manager needs to undertake.

As a Facility Manager, your first task is therefore to ensure that your colleagues know you. If they don't know you, they won't know what you stand for and what you can contribute, and they will not take your objectives into account, nor you theirs. But it doesn't stop with just the colleagues you have to approach: you need to make sure that all employees know you and your department, and understand your added value. They need to know what they can approach FM for.

Ideally, this should be made clear to them as soon as they start at the company, for example, by presenting them with a delightful experience when they come to the office, starting with the charging station they can reserve upon arrival at the office, followed by picking up a delicious cappuccino from the barista, and then attending a welcome meeting in a perfectly heated, well lit, and ventilated meeting room. But you also guide them to answers to specific questions: are there shared cars, what do I do when I forget my badge, etc. If you can take on your role here as well, you will quickly become a visible and appreciated player in the organisation. At the same time, you also need to become known at the C-level. They need to be aware of the business issues you can add value to. Make sure they are informed, either by joining the management meetings yourself or by having them explained and advocated by your manager who does attend the table.

Getting to know you is the first step, the next step is for them to learn to appreciate and like you. You can reach this 'like' phase by being as positive and constructive as possible. Therefore, make sure you are always findable and visible. Ensure that your 'tone of voice' matches the company's vision and values. Help people quickly and efficiently when they come to complain about a meeting room being too hot, not enough coffee, or a non-reserved workspace, but also don't lose your smile in the process. You are, in a way, the host for all 'guests', the employees you want to provide with the most pleasant work experience possible. Oh yes, and when you have solved a problem perfectly, don't forget to share this 'success' with everyone. Positive stories always do well on the intranet. And so, gradually, all colleagues will come to appreciate you even more.

This creates a positive spiral: Everyone gets to know and appreciate FM better and better, and as a result, they increasingly use your services. Gradually, a bond of trust is formed, which elevates the conversation to a higher level.

THE FOUNDATIONS OF TEAMWORK

To optimise FM and achieve all intended objectives, strong teamwork is essential. Not just within the FM department, but also with other departments. You will need to work together as one large team to achieve these results, as they are almost always cross-departmental.

This all starts with mutual trust. If there is sufficient trust, people dare to engage in conflict with each other to achieve the best possible result. This also increases involvement in the joint project, as everyone knows that their voice matters. Increased involvement leads to a higher sense of responsibility. And this, in turn, leads to better results.

Therefore, I would like to offer the following advice to achieve and maintain top results:
- Create a safe environment where you can speak and collaborate. Where team members help each other and the strengths of the team are further emphasised.
- If there are issues, address and discuss them immediately.
- Make practical arrangements and solutions.
- Gather input from the involved team and try to avoid political games.
- Ensure you have buy-in and alignment on the common objectives.
- Ensure a clear 'why' (direction) and define priorities.
- Monitor the weaker performers and hold them 'accountable'. The same standards must apply to ALL team members.

The above is based on Lencioni's book "The Five Dysfunctions of a Team".

Above, we outlined how FM and the workplace experience can be put on the map and how to do this. Here we address how we can put this into a simple set of questions. What do we need to achieve success?

1. What do you need for your own work?
2. What do you need from your team?
3. What do you need from your direct manager?
4. What do you need from the C-level?
5. What do you need from your end customers, the employees?

To optimally align your objectives with those of other departments and colleagues, a great deal of discussion is required. Not only about the concrete objective facts and figures but also about what others actually want. This poses a challenge for many Facility Managers: they are very strong in process and project management to achieve those objectives but often lose sight of the 'iceberg principle'. This principle states that the objective, measurable, factual, and rational aspects only form a fraction of the decision-making process. Those who do not take into account what is playing out beneath the surface, the largest part of the iceberg, will often fail in aligning the objectives. The colleagues' beliefs, their standards and values, the general company culture but also the individual character: All this and much more determines how people think, feel, and decide on their own and the general objectives.

Figure 5.2: The workplace iceberg.

RABOBANK: TEAMWORK MAKES THE DIFFERENCE IN A CHALLENGING PROJECT

A prime example of the importance of teamwork in FM is seen in the Rabo@ Anywhere project of the Dutch multi-national Rabobank. This 125-year-old bank, employing 46,000 staff across 36 countries, has its headquarters located in Utrecht, in the so-called Rabo Central House. This building, being the largest location of the bank with 5,300 workstations, was one of the buildings involved in the project.

Jan Nieuweboer

With Rabo@Anywhere, the bank aimed to find the best way of hybrid working. This quest had started before the Covid pandemic but accelerated due to the mandatory remote work during that period. To optimise this quest, several drastic decisions were made.

The most notable of these perfectly illustrates how FM yields the best results when it is part of a larger whole within the organisation, says Jan Nieuweboer, Senior Consultant on hybrid working at Rabobank: "A very deliberate choice was made to approach this project 'cross-organisationally'. HR, FM, IT, Risk, Communication, and others had to come together because all aspects are necessary to make this a success." The success of this cross-functional team even led to a reorganisation of the entire HR organisation two years ago: "FM, HR, and ICT for the workplace now all work together in a new department, named CHRO. The old silos have disappeared and have been replaced by 'tribes'. Our work is now much more employee- and experience-oriented."

This collaboration has also led to several other successful choices. For instance, the joint team decided to conduct a 'scientific' experiment in the initial phase (2020 and early 2021), said Jan Nieuweboer: "We tested two different work environments, each for three target groups. One work environment was very similar to the traditional work environment of the past, the other was very innovative with, among other things, many new digital tools. The findings were very enlightening. People in the new environment, regardless of their role, started to reflect more on their way of working and began to approach things differently. The other group more or less fell back on the old way of working. Hence, the physical environment and the digital tools you provide very much determine your willingness to work differently." This learning curve was very decisive for the rest of the project. And it led to a positive business case to continue the transformation of the work environment.

The willingness to let the course of the project be determined by the results of this experiment also illustrates how open the project team has been from the outset. "We never started with the obligation to come to the office, but wanted to examine on a team by team basis what the needs and expectations were, also in terms of customer contacts. We also looked into how other banks are dealing with this. And this has certainly led, in the case of the London office, to increased retention and attraction of new employees."

The further rollout after the first pilot projects has led to a thorough revision of the workplace. Notably, the project team mainly focused on the impact on the work experience, and the physical reorganisation was included in a more traditional FM project. But at the same time, the FM team was very involved in aligning infrastructure with all employee needs, as individuals and as a team. "We also only made adjustments where necessary," Jan adds. "Investments were made to replace the screens in the meeting rooms with screens that are MS Teams-certified and have a camera and speakers onboard. And almost all 'refurbishments' are based on recycled material. This way, we lower our carbon footprint and keep costs manageable."

The project Rabo@Anywhere has a set duration, with the first one and a half years mainly devoted to designing and experimenting. "From the end of 2023 to the end of 2024, the full rollout must happen with full focus on the employee journey and experience," confirms Jan Nieuweboer, "but we are already reaping the benefits of the project. 95% of our people do not want to go back to the old way of working. Hybrid working has become the norm. That has been a tremendous success. Not only is satisfaction and well-being higher than ever, but the bank has also been able to save a lot of costs. The digital tools allow for improved efficiency of the hybrid teams. And trust in management and in each other has greatly increased, even with the decreased physical presence."

Thus, there is satisfaction all around for the project team of Rabo@Anywhere. Jan is also happy to share some tips with those now wanting to start such a project: "What really helped a lot was the extensive measuring and collection of data for thorough preliminary research. That was definitely a key to success. Also, the choice to involve employees from the start of the project made a difference. People also received feedback and insight into what needed to be done in as short a time as possible. Communication was crucial in this. Then you see the power of a cross-functional team: collaboration within this team is an essential condition for success."

7 STEPS TO SUCCESS

The conclusion of this chapter is crystal clear: Only if you move away from the island culture of the past, can you as a Facility Manager achieve your intended results. A Facility Manager must be a bridge-builder, who ensures connection between departments to work together on the common business objectives. To further put your FM department on the map, but also and especially to reach the best result for your company together with other departments, you need to take the following steps:

1. Determine where you create added value at an operational, tactical, and strategic level.
2. Do your stakeholder management (HR/IT/FIN/...).
3. Take care of your own marketing (know-like-trust).
4. Optimise teamwork in your FM team.
5. Align your objectives with your colleagues and vice versa.
6. Map both processes and emotional parameters and make use of your own company iceberg principle.
7. Repeat the previous six steps with sufficient regularity. An organisation is subject to continuous change.

CHAPTER 6

HAPPY EMPLOYEES ARE HAPPY TO STAY

F M and workplace experience are inextricably linked; this has become clear by now. But to be able to build that optimal workplace experience, it's also crucial to understand exactly what employees desire, what they need. In this respect, our profession closely aligns with Human Resources (HR), with the team that constantly works on the well-being and job satisfaction of all the talent present.

I don't need to tell you: At some point everyone has entered an office where the desolation nearly drips from the walls. The kind of office that makes your heart sink when you see the enclosed spaces with stacks of paper everywhere. I vowed never to have to work in such an environment. Even if you don't understand the mechanisms behind it, you just feel there's a direct link between the management and layout of the workplace on one hand and the well-being and job satisfaction of the employees on the other. I've experienced it myself multiple times: When the click between your norms and values and those of the company is gone, it becomes difficult to continue together. And the company's vision of the workplace cannot be seen independently of this.

But as a Facility Manager, you don't want to rely solely on this feeling; you also want to thoroughly understand how exactly this connection works, to then be able to work with it as effectively as possible. By paying attention to employees and incorporating those learnings into a clear structural policy on well-being, we can ensure vital, engaged, and healthy employees. Employees who are happy at work, in turn, ensure that the results are achieved. To realise this, it is important that there is good cooperation between the various stakeholders who all contribute to the well-being of employees from their domain of expertise: Facility Managers who are responsible for the best possible workplace environment on the one hand, but also HR managers, who know better than anyone else exactly what those employees are looking for.

Kathleen Louckx

It seemed obvious to me to seek HR expertise to enrich this chapter. It was no coincidence that I did not have to look long for a suitable conversation partner: Kathleen Louckx is an HR expert who has specialised in well-being, job satisfaction, and all other aspects that are important to employees. Not coincidental at all, because Kathleen is not only an excellent HR expert and Chief of Happiness & Well-being, she is also my – excellent – wife. Therefore, I thank her not only for her support during the writing of this book, but also in this chapter for her valuable substantive contributions and insights.

In this chapter, we start with providing insight into psychosocial risks. Once that foundation is laid, we can delve deeper into my perception of the three dimensions of job satisfaction. And how do we get into a flow to achieve optimal results? To do this, I engaged in a conversation with Jonas De Kerf from KU Leuven. Building teamwork and engagement in the workplace is definitely something we can facilitate, right? As a use case, we take Ageas with their new head office in Brussels. And what could be handier to conclude with than a simple checklist to align well-being and the workplace?

LEGAL FRAMEWORK: PREVENTING PSYCHOSOCIAL RISKS

Ensuring the well-being of employees is not just a noble goal or a weapon in the battle for talent; it is also a legal obligation imposed both nationally and at the European level. Every employer is required to implement a well-being policy based on general principles (preventing risks, eliminating or reducing them at the source, providing training and information to employees). This policy must be integrated into the entire management of the company. Regulations regarding the prevention of psychosocial risks at work need to be drawn up, including stress, violence, bullying, and unwanted sexual behaviour at work.

Initially, this concerns health and safety at work. However, broader attention is also paid to psychosocial risks that need to be contained or even prevented. Psychosocial risks at work include professional risks that can cause psychological and possibly also physical harm to employees. They can also impact safety on the work floor and the proper functioning of companies. The employer must take necessary measures to prevent psychosocial risks at work, to prevent the damage resulting from these risks, or to limit this damage.

Upon closer examination, it is evident that psychosocial risks can be found at many levels:

- **The work organisation**: The structure of the organisation (horizontal – vertical), the division of tasks, work procedures, management tools, management style, and the general policy conducted in the company.
- **The content of work:** The tasks of the employee. The content of work includes, among other things, the complexity and variation of tasks, the emotional burden (interactions with the public, contact with suffering, etc.), the psychological burden (linked to, among other things, the difficulty of tasks), the physical burden, and the clarity of tasks.
- **The working conditions**: Everything related to the modalities of the execution of the work relationship, such as the nature of the agreement and the type of work schedule (night work, shift work, atypical hours, etc.), training opportunities, career management, and evaluation procedures.
- **Interpersonal relationships at work**: The internal relationships (among employees, with one's direct manager, with the hierarchical structure, etc.), and relationships with third parties, the opportunities for contact, communication, etc. The quality of conditions for work relationships (cooperation, integration, etc.) also falls under this category.
- **The working conditions**: The material environment in which the work is performed, such as the layout of the workplace, the working tools, noise, lighting, substances used, and work postures.

It is evident that, especially at the last evel - working conditions -, FM can play a major role. But the Facility Manager can also play a role in optimising labour relations, by providing a work environment that can facilitate and improve relationships between colleagues, with the customer, and with management.

ARAMCO: HOW TO ENSURE THE WELL-BEING OF OVER 70,000 EMPLOYEES

Aramco, the world-leading energy and oil supplier headquartered in Saudi Arabia, employs over 70,000 people worldwide. It seems an impossible task, yet Aramco aims for every employee to feel their well-being is taken care of, so they can perform their best at work and help the company remain productive and profitable. Here is a glimpse into how they specifically tackle this.

Paul Burgess

"Just like other organisations, the pandemic really highlighted the necessity for us to be conscious of well-being," says Paul Burgess, Global Employee Well-being Program Lead at Aramco. "In 2021, we developed a well-being strategy, where the first tangible initiative was a set of well-being questions, integrated into our employee engagement survey. The responses and insights from the employees served as a starting point to know where to focus our programme to enhance our employees' well-being, which ultimately could make Aramco the 'best place to work'."

Aramco defines well-being as "the state of one's life through good physical, emotional, social, and occupational health, happiness, and satisfaction with clear goals and aspirations". This definition is represented by nine dimensions of well-being: Purpose, Emotional, Intellectual, Social, Environmental, Digital, Physical, Financial, and Occupational well-being. The goal is to give every employee a 'purpose' (a reason to work), with every effort made to avoid or reduce stress, increase resilience, and improve the well-being of employees. There are ample opportunities for learning and knowledge sharing, and workplaces are made as pleasant as possible. "We pay a lot of attention to this," Paul assures us.

To bring the well-being and workplace strategy to life, Aramco has a Global Well-being Programme designed to offer specific services to their employees, including individual assessments and activities through campaigns, company challenges, and awards. Moreover, the well-being programme offers leadership and champions training (ambassadors) along with extensive resources, including toolkits and learning channels. "The programme is part of a broader employee experience, as we recognise the importance of focusing on improving the workplace employee experience, so our employees can be more engaged and experience better well-being," explains Paul.

"We invest a lot of time and energy in training and supporting our leaders," added Paul, "with campaigns and communication plans for leadership programmes, so our leaders have the tools and insights to assist their team members. Regarding employee engagement, we listen to our employees through engagement surveys and have a 'championship' programme with key figures in the workplace, who can share the vision and engage colleagues." The strategic aim is to bring everyone together around the same goal: a "healthy employee population". "Employees have access to e-learning and other forms of self-development, and are given advice and support around self-care and a healthy lifestyle. Being in an industrial setting, safety is naturally a key concern. Last but not least, there is clear governance around well-being, so everyone realises the whole company stands behind this initiative," says Paul.

The working environment plays a significant role in this well-being narrative in many ways, he notes: "By collaborating with internal stakeholders, we can respond to the specific needs of the diverse talent, to create a healthy working environment." Facilities Management helps ensure Aramco becomes a safe, stress-free environment where well-being is not an empty concept, but a strategic goal for the company, as they strive to make Saudi Aramco the employer of choice and the 'Best Place' to work not only in the Kingdom of Saudi Arabia but also globally!

Taking care of the well-being and satisfaction of employees is not just a legal obligation. After all, workplace happiness has a clear ROI (Return on Investment), in the form of reduced absenteeism, lower turnover, higher productivity, and better business outcomes. But we also see improvements in terms of collaboration, efficiency, a better work atmosphere, the health and self-development of employees, and an increase in energy and vitality of employees. Investing in a strategic and practical approach pays off; it is a WIN-WIN-WIN for individual employees, the team, and the organisation.

As an organisation, you can contribute to this at various levels. You can work on innovation and creativity, leadership, diversity and inclusion, you can promote team dynamics and improve interpersonal relations, and ensure greater job satisfaction. However, if you lose sight of work-related factors – such as ergonomics and health, flexibility, and work-life balance – you will only partially achieve satisfaction, well-being, and happiness. It is also important to address these at all times, not just when times are tough. The workplace is the foundation of every effort to make employees happy within their work environment. And you achieve that happiness only if you engage employees on various levels.

BRAIN, BELONGING, AND BALANCE: THE THREE DIMENSIONS OF EMPLOYEE HAPPINESS

If you aim to keep employees satisfied and happy in their work environment, you must consider the various facets of an employee. For this purpose, we use the so-called 3 Bs: brain, belonging, and balance. When you address all three dimensions, you will notice that your employees are more motivated, where we can make the connection to work happiness.

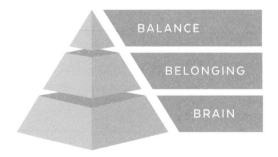

Figure 6.1: The 3 dimensions of employee happiness.

As the basis of the above illustration, we talk about **'brain'**. **Brain stands for the fulfilment of our job satisfaction**, the rational and functional aspects, job content, job fulfilment, working conditions, work tools, and a safe working environment; in short, the foundation for the well-being, satisfaction, and performance of employees. If this foundation is not stable, it is difficult to focus on the next important facets that contribute to the work happiness of employees. To satisfy employees in this regard, as a Facility Manager you can focus on a customised workplace that ensures that everyone can perform their work as optimally as possible in their own way.

Another important facet is the emotional aspect, say, the heart of the employee. We call this **'belonging'**, the feeling of belonging, the connection with team members, supervisors, and the organisation. For this purpose, work is being done on the connection between employees, on team dynamics, but also on corporate culture and values, the work atmosphere where we make agreements on how we treat each other, so that employees can identify themselves.

Finally, we need to consider the last **'balance'**, namely the balance between work and private life, but also between energy givers and energy drainers. This involves paying necessary attention to flexibility of and for employees: physical and mental health, work-private life, ergonomics and health, stress, flexibility etc. In short: the 'well-being' of employees is central here.

All three facets of the employee should be kept in mind when developing your FM strategy. Previously, the focus was mainly on the rational aspect, the 'brain' of the employee. But since the Covid pandemic, it has become clear to everyone how important this balance has become for employees, and also how much they long for that feeling of belonging. We will go into each of these three facets in more detail later.

BRAIN: HOW DO YOU GET (KEEP) EMPLOYEES 'IN THE FLOW'?

In my search for workable models to map the functional impact of the work environment on productivity and well-being of employees, I came into contact with Jonas De Kerf, a researcher at KU Leuven. He is specifically investigating how and when employees get 'in the flow' as the subject of his doctoral thesis.

Jonas De Kerf

"In the 70s and 80s, research in our field primarily focused on the relationship between labour and reward. But gradually, there was a growing realisation that this did not explain why a lot of people sometimes work hard without any reward attached to it," explains Jonas. This is especially clear with hobbies and sports; people put in tremendous effort without necessarily being rewarded. "Think about rock climbing," Jonas gives as an example, "it's damn hard work and yet many people are drawn to it. When you ask them why, the word 'flow' often comes up: people get into the flow and want to stay there, although they can't immediately explain why it feels so good."

Although the flow is mainly known in a sports context, we also see this phenomenon in the work environment. Jonas continues: "Those moments of supreme concentration on a challenging task can be described as 'getting into the flow': all the concerns of your extensive to-do list at work, picking up the children, etc., suddenly disappear into the background and you lose yourself completely in this task. It gives you a boost in that moment, but also afterwards, when you see how much work you have done in that flow."

To reach that flow, you need to be able to concentrate for a long period. So, it's important to have a work environment where this concentration is not constantly broken. Are you de facto more often 'in the flow' at home than in the office? "Not necessarily," replies Jonas, "some people get into the flow better with others around them. Then you can even get into a sort of 'team flow', when many are concentrating at the same time. And you can also have 'flow moments' during meetings. It is very much dependent on the person and the context."

What then are the conditions for getting employees 'in the flow'? According to Jonas, there are three key conditions: "On the one hand, there's the task itself: it needs to be sufficiently challenging and interesting, so not a routine task. On the other hand, the environment must provide the right conditions: the right level of privacy, auditory and visual stimuli (sufficiently lit but also quiet spaces, depending on who thrives best in which conditions). But you also need to know and estimate yourself well. Some people get into the flow better in the morning, so they should ideally hold their meetings in the afternoon, when they are less easily in the flow."

As a company, you therefore need to strive for the right environments to be able to realise that flow, but also to interrupt the flow occasionally: "No one can stay in the flow uninterrupted for eight hours; it's important to plan breaks in time to recharge your batteries."

For the Facility Manager, this means that work needs to be done on various facets, Jonas concludes: "You need to provide a workplace where every type of task is possible, including those for which employees want to get into the flow. That means removing distracting factors but also providing an area with fixed workplaces for the creatures of habit that we are. And striving for that ideal mix that supports every possible task. Because a workday consists of more than just flow tasks." Each employee then chooses for themselves which task they will perform when. Finally, Jonas has this advice for employees: "Choose which tasks you will perform, choose the most suitable location and time for this, and how long you will spend on it. Don't make it too short and not too long: somewhere between 1 and 3 hours is usually advisable."

As we discussed extensively in chapter 3, the challenge for Facility Managers goes beyond taking into account the expectations of the average employee. Since the percentage of employees with some form of neurodiversity can be high in an average organisation, it is not only socially responsible to take this into account but also a matter of sound business sense. This group is simply too important to overlook as we strive for an optimal working environment for every employee.

BELONGING: BUILDING TEAMWORK AND ENGAGEMENT

Leaders have a significant influence on how their employees feel when they come to work. In a healthy team, everyone can work efficiently and happily when there's a focus on trust, respect, appreciation, support, diversity and inclusion, relationships, growth, results, and successes. Through their support to the team, leaders create a culture within which employees feel engaged, can grow, and achieve their successes. In this way, they play a crucial role in forming a positive employee experience and the development and retention of their staff.

As a leader, it is important to find the right balance between relationship & result. You won't achieve the right results if you don't focus on your employees. Ensure a correct, positive, and informal relationship with your employees. But employees themselves can also make a very large contribution to positive relationships at the workplace. Organisations can support employees as much as possible by creating a context, a framework that promotes the right connection and communication skills, and fosters trust, appreciation, and collaboration within teams. In other words: the organisation supports its employees and provides them with the tools for optimal teamwork.

The importance of the right communication cannot be overstated. And the right communication sometimes means no communication at all. In the past, the emphasis was too often on always being reachable. However, this 'always on' mentality can contribute to stress for employees, as is now sufficiently known. Companies would do well to work on disconnection among their workers: teaching them that it is okay, even advisable, to disconnect, to not immediately respond to every email, to not slavishly answer every phone call. There is a time and a place for synchronous communication and asynchronous communication. And Facility Managers can play a significant role in this.

A TIME AND PLACE FOR SYNCHRONOUS AND ASYNCHRONOUS COMMUNICATION

Synchronous communication is 'real-time' communication where all parties involved are available simultaneously, such as telephone calls and video conferences. It is a direct form of communication where participants can immediately respond to messages. Asynchronous communication means that there can and may be a delay between sending and receiving messages, and participants can respond when it suits them. This is the case with emails, forum posts, text messages, recorded videos and voicemails. FM plays a crucial role in facilitating both synchronous and asynchronous communication in the workplace.

For synchronous communication, FM can provide well-equipped meeting rooms with the necessary **technological infrastructure**, such as video conferencing systems, screens, and audio equipment. This ensures that teams can communicate effectively, even if they are in different locations. Additionally, Facility Managers can facilitate all forms of face-to-face communication, with **open workspaces** for more interaction between employees **and/or enclosed spaces** for more privacy during meetings. And for virtual real-time communication, FM and IT are responsible for the **availability and functionality of communication technologies** such as phone systems and instant messaging platforms.

For asynchronous communication, FM and IT can contribute to setting up effective **intranet platforms and information systems**. This gives employees the opportunity to look up important information, such as policy documents, announcements, and news, whenever it suits them. By **streamlining workflows and processes**, FM can create an environment where employees can share and receive information in a structured and organised manner. **Facilitating flexible workspaces and supporting remote work opportunities** can contribute to asynchronous communication. This gives employees the freedom to work at times that best fit their individual schedules. Finally, Facility Managers can contribute to **educating employees on effective asynchronous communication practices**, which may include promoting good email habits, the use of collaborative tools, and being mindful of time zones.

How does this relate to the famous **'digital detox'**? *

By engaging in a digital detox, we can relearn how to disconnect from our devices, interact with our digital lives more consciously and in a more balanced way, and establish healthier boundaries with technology. This applies to the workplace as well! The risk is that employees become excessively dependent on the 'always on' mentality. The digital evolution allows us to access more information in less time, but this exchange of information now knows no limits. Digital overload is increasingly present, and it's important that you learn to consciously deal with the amount of information you receive, that you are aware of the use of digital tools, and that you timeously schedule a moment for rest.

Give your brain some well-deserved rest by not bombarding it with extra stimuli and new information. This is not only good for the brain, but your physical body will be very thankful for it. Find the right way to move from digital overload to digital comfort. Give your brain the time and space to rest, to promote relaxation. You get the most out of a digital detox when you see it as an opportunity to develop new habits and to interact differently with digital communication tools. This teaches you to maintain a better balance between your offline and online 'life'.

---

* Source: E-book: Digital Detox for more work happiness from Tryangle

As a manager of a company, you can also play a very important role in this. Make agreements within your company and/or your team regarding availability. Who needs to be available when? Which communication tool is for what purpose, what are the exceptions for urgent matters, and how do we handle that? How do we communicate with each other about who is in focus time when?

Limit the number of digital communication tools on the workplace floor. Communicating is often not the core business of most employees but mainly a means to perform tasks. Employees can get lost in the amount of information and channels if email, WhatsApp, Teams, internal chat, intranet, etc., are used and need to be followed up. Each communication tool requires skills, agreements, time, and energy.

A handy tool in this context can be the communication matrix below. Make a distinction between urgent and non-urgent communication and between important and unimportant communication.

Figure 6.2: The communication matrix.

FM can play a key role in promoting digital detox in the workplace by creating an environment that encourages healthy digital habits. Ensure a working environment where work can be done with focus. Every little ping from your smartphone causes a break in your attention. Sometimes you may not even notice it, but your brain picks it up and unconsciously decides what to do with that stimulus. Your concentration is weakened for a moment, and it inevitably requires extra energy to get back into the same flow.

Open offices can also be a source of overstimulation for employees; offer them the possibility to sit separately and use your hybrid work policy to allow employees to complete a task in peace. For example, by setting up Digital Free Zones, specific areas in the workplace where digital devices are not allowed. Or provide spaces where employees can retreat for rest and silence. In these quiet rooms, digital devices are not allowed, giving employees the chance to concentrate and be away from constant digital stimuli.

Facility Managers can encourage digital detox at various levels. You can establish a culture in which employees are encouraged to take healthy breaks during their workday, completely disconnecting from digital devices. This can improve concentration and productivity. But you can also implement technological solutions that make it possible to temporarily limit access to certain digital tools. This can make it easier for employees to adhere to digital breaks. By integrating all these approaches, FM can contribute to a culture of digital awareness and balance in the workplace, providing employees with the necessary space to disconnect and promote their well-being.

BALANCE IS ESSENTIAL FOR WELL-BEING

Stress and increased workload can lead to decreased productivity and absenteeism. These are factors that must constantly be addressed. However, working on well-being really works when it transcends the curative approach of combatting pressure and stress, and everyone actively and preventively deals with well-being and stress-related complaints. Well-being in the workplace is a complex and dynamic concept that encompasses the physical, mental, emotional, and social health and satisfaction of employees. A corporate well-being approach combines all the information and tools a company can provide, pouring them into a suitable action plan and a well-being policy to optimise well-being at work and make it sustainable and effective.

A good policy guides employees around well-being, resilience, and vitality, finds the right balance between work and private life, and tailors this to the company culture. It boosts employees' resilience against stress and increased workload, ensuring they become aware of their own energy givers and takers so they can also intervene proactively if the balance is compromised.

As a Facility Manager, you can support this policy in various ways. You can provide a clear hybrid working policy, encourage people to take the stairs instead of the elevator, organise sports and running events, offer well-being training and much more. And don't forget the fruit basket, as this was a standard solution offered by FM in the past. I make a little joke about it, just give them a fruit basket and you can tick the box for the well-being bulletpoint. But all this only adds value if there is already sufficient focus on good job satisfaction (brain) and the right connection (belonging) with and within the company.

IF YOU BUILD IT, THEY WILL WORK. IT'S NOT THAT SIMPLE

Anton Maes

On the topic of 'FM and well-being,' I found a great conversation partner in Anton Maes. Not only is he a board member at IFMA Belgium and the We-Hub (Workplace Evolutionaries) leader for Belgium, but he also has a background in psychology, making him excellently placed to bridge both worlds. Additionally, he is the inspiration behind the consultancy firm brainmove, which guides organisations in developing an optimal workplace strategy.

Anton pointed out several incorrect perceptions that often exist around this topic. For example, it is often unabashedly assumed that there is a direct, linear relationship between well-being and performance: "In other words: we provide our employees with a new, fun working environment, they all become 'happy', and they start working like crazy. Of course, it's not that simple! Well-being varies greatly from person to person. Scientific research indicates that the relationship between well-being and productivity is influenced by a whole range of variables such as the quality of leadership, social connection, job satisfaction, emotional health, and physical health."

But no one disputes the basic principle that we must offer a context in which our employees can give their best in the best possible conditions. Some interventions, such as providing sit-stand furniture, are a nice illustration of this principle. Employees change their sitting posture throughout the day, thus preventing physical complaints, ensuring variation, and optimising output.

Many organisations have started to question their offices in the aftermath of the Covid crisis. This is a necessary, healthy, and sustainable reflex. But to simply assume that the workplace of the future will only be used as a trendy meeting environment is probably too simplistic. Not all users will systematically do their concentration work at home in the future. This may be due to their profile; some professions, such as experts, lawyers, etc., mainly do concentration work and thus also need a quiet working environment at work. The personal preference of users is also important here. Some people will simply prefer to come to the office for every professional activity. They need the social interaction or want to keep work and home strictly separate. It is not easy to influence and change this. Yet, you already see some organisations opting for a 'remote first' approach and promoting this as a benefit in kind on the labour market.

Another incorrect perception is that a beautiful and fitting work environment is the key to success in increasing the well-being and productivity of employees. Indeed, the work environment must be of high quality and offer the right types of workspaces to be successful. However, this is not enough. Here too, an important balance plays a role, namely between the quality of the work environment and the behaviour of users. A wonderful work environment can be completely spoiled if users do not adjust their behaviour. They start meetings in the open-plan office, they make calls unashamedly between workspaces, or they leave their materials at the flexible workspaces because they will be sitting there again the next day. To achieve successful collaboration in the activity-based work environment, we must also change the behaviour of users, and this often does not happen without a struggle.

We often hear that people are creatures of habit and do not want to, sometimes even cannot, change their behaviour. However, that too is a myth. With proper guidance through a change process, but also by offering a context that will spontaneously support the desired behaviour, we can go a long way. Are you planning to loudly discuss your weekend in the local public library? I didn't think so. If we offer a quiet space in the new work environment that gives the feeling of a library, and where the agreement is that everyone works there in silence, then you can also work quietly at the office without isolating yourself. You just need the right infrastructure and the right agreements.

Finally, Anton also emphasises the importance of mature leadership in the organisation. The Covid pandemic has forced many leaders to experiment with new forms of leadership. While in the past, the activities of the team could be easily monitored and controlled due to physical proximity and visibility, the manager had to learn to collaborate with the team from a distance. For this, they also had to take on new roles, such as the role of coach, leader, and entrepreneur. Teams that work remotely enjoy significantly greater freedom. Employees plan their own day and determine when they will take on which tasks. "The manager must transform into a facilitator who guides the team to maximum output based on trust. Here, maintaining a good balance between controlling and coaching is crucial," concludes Anton. Well-being and balance are yet again inseparably linked.

'AN IMPORTANT BALANCE PLAYS A ROLE, NAMELY BETWEEN THE QUALITY OF THE WORK ENVIRONMENT AND THE BEHAVIOUR OF THE USERS. A WONDERFUL WORK ENVIRONMENT CAN BE COMPLETELY SPOILED IF USERS DO NOT ADJUST THEIR BEHAVIOUR.'

AGEAS

A good example of how an organisation can make a success of an FM project is found at the international insurance group Ageas. In their strategic HR plan, named 'Great Place to Grow', they explored ways to reunite their people but in a better and smarter way, under the motto 'Smarter Together'. For this, they also relied on the lessons learned during the Covid pandemic.

Eddy Debrulle

The first pillar was the clear agreements on hybrid working, explains Eddy Debrulle, Group HR Director at Ageas: "It had to be a solid system for employ-ees with the necessary flexibility too. Nothing is mandatory, but we do follow the principle: the customer comes first, then the team, and only then personal preferences. The mindset is more important than too many rules."

The second pillar was the new building. "The previous office was outdated," says Eddy, "and based on a number of criteria such as location and accessibility, we ended up at the Manhattan Center in the heart of Brussels. For the design, attention was paid not only to design but also to technology, well-being, comfort, and mobility, including adjustable office equipment. In parallel, we also invested in the home office environment: screens, office chairs, and speakers must offer the home worker the opportunity to work as comfortably and productively as at the office."

The digital infrastructure was a key pillar for the success of the project, says Eddy: "The digital accessibility throughout the entire office and the many meeting rooms with all the necessary audiovisual tools have made a significant contribution to the transition to hybrid and 'paperless' working. But we were especially impressed by the speed with which our employees embraced all this."

This brings us to the fourth and final pillar: change management. "Not an easy task," admits Eddy: "How can you motivate employees to come to the new building?" To get everyone on board, a 'sounding board' was established, consisting of one to two participants from each department. Their input, for example about the mix of individual spaces and open spaces, was indeed taken into account in the final decision, Eddy assures us: "We wanted a good mix between our own input and the design and project team. An extensive communication trajectory was also set up with photos, videos, monitoring of work, etc. Feedback meetings with 'people management' were also held regularly. Naturally, you encounter resistance, which you have to listen to, but you must stick to the set lines and philosophy of the project. The hybrid way of working is a big adjustment for 'people managers' and a continuous change process towards a new interpretation of their responsibilities."

The sounding board, the continuous involvement of people from every department, proved to be a key factor in the success of this project, Eddy says: "They were the perfect ambassadors for the new building. But the cosy and homely decor also plays a role, of course. As does the choice for high-quality materials. Moreover, the decision to have sufficient coffee corners should not be underestimated, just like the availability of a fitness room and bike parking in the multitenant building of the Manhattan Center." Eddy also points out the muted acoustics and the lighting that adjusts to the outside light. "Finally, I am convinced that our opening day, the festive moment we experienced together, contributed to acceptance among colleagues."

Of course, there are also challenges, Eddy admits: "For example, we wonder how the group dynamics will change now that we have moved from 1 to 4 floors. But with our Cube, the open central space with a magnificent view of Brussels which is not only a pleasant meeting place for our people but from where everyone can go to the other floors via the majestic spiral staircase, we have a good trump card."

That the focus on sustainability has paid off can be objectively substantiated with certificates such as the BREAAM excellent certificate for the building and the WELL build certificate, Eddy says, "but we only really knew we had succeeded in this after the opening day when everyone came to say it exceeded all expectations. And certainly in the days and weeks after, when more people came to the office than we had hoped. Fortunately, we have provided a user-friendly tool to reserve workspaces."

THE MINDSET IS MORE IMPORTANT THAN TOO MANY RULES.

Eddy gladly shares the main lessons he learned during this project as a tip for the readers: "Take the time to prepare well. Choose partners who understand your company, what you stand for and where you are heading. Involve all stakeholders very quickly but also stick to the guidelines you have drawn up. Ensure top management is on board and that you have enough autonomy to give approvals. Make things visual, show them to people instead of writing long memos or emails. Lastly: know who your ambassadors are and deploy them fully!"

CORPORATE BRANDING

Those who make an effort to create an optimal work environment that enhances productivity and a sense of belonging, and also make it maximally possible for employees' balance and well-being, naturally get an organisation to be proud of. On the one hand, your own employees will continue to work happily for your organisation; on the other hand, you have an excellent tool to attract new talent. Your company becomes literally more attractive, not just in terms of form and design but also as an employer that understands the needs of its employees and responds to them. This could be about the amount of teleworking but also about the location and other aspects of mobility such as car sharing. All these are aspects where the Facility Manager must also play a role. Thus, the Facility Manager helps make the workplace a strategic weapon. And this on many levels: identity and values, hospitality and customer orientation, ESG, well-being, technology, and innovation. In short, a company where talent is eager to come and even more eager to stay.

A HANDY CHECKLIST

Can't wait to get started with the insights above? But are you first looking for a good way to show your team or colleagues how FM, the workplace, and employee well-being are viewed? Then you actually don't need much. Using your hand as a checklist can take you a long way.

I like to use this 'technical' aid when it comes to the HR aspects of FM. Each finger stands for one major question, which can then be divided into sub-questions. Specifically, it looks like this:
- Thumb: What is the top quality of your workplace?
- Index finger: What are the expectations of the workplace?
- Middle finger: What do we not want in the workplace?
- Ring finger: How do we feel connected to the workplace?
- Pinky finger: How do you want to grow in your workplace; where do you want to grow?

If you have an answer to all these questions and the corresponding sub-questions, you already have a good basis to align your FM strategy.

Figure 6.3: A handy checklist.

7 STEPS TO SUCCESS

1. Assemble your stakeholder team within your organisation. It's all about the people; involve employees – brain, heart, belonging, and balance.
2. Determine your FM role in the psychosocial risks within your organisation.
3. How do you get your colleagues more 'in the flow'?
4. What does your synchronous and asynchronous communication look like? Focus on digital detox.
5. Guide your employees; take them by the hand through your workplace concept.
6. Determine your corporate branding.
7. Use your handy checklist.

CHAPTER 7

SUSTAINABILITY LASTS THE LONGEST

S ustainable and environmentally conscious business practices are not a recent
trend, but it is only in the past decade that they have truly risen to the top of
every organisation's agenda. I still remember how, as a young lad in Melsele,
a small village in East Flanders not far from Antwerp, I could see the port of Antwerp in the distance. Being the second largest port in Europe, it was, of course,
always bustling with activity, and I could spend hours marvelling at all the lights,
ships, and chimneys with impressive plumes of smoke and vapours. It was only
many years later that my admiration for that logistical giant gradually gave way
to different feelings. I began to wonder if all those vapours and less visible substances were healthy for those who worked there and for those who lived nearby,
like ourselves. Today, there are enough parties alerting us to this, and not least
the companies themselves. Business operations must become more sustainable,
environmentally aware, and socially responsible, and those who do not comply
will sooner or later be presented with the bill.

For FM, ESG (Environmental, Sustainable, Governance) has also become a top priority. But in reality, sustainability has always played a prominent role within FM.
However, when we used to talk about energy-efficient buildings in the past, the
emphasis was mainly on 'efficient'. The goal was to keep costs as low as possible.
It was only later that a real concern for the environment was added. A logical evolution, in my opinion: the realisation that there is no planet B forces us all to be
more conscious of how we treat our earth. Musk may still believe that we will one
day colonise Mars, but for the majority, it's clear that we're better off taking care
of what we already have. And so, concepts like 'renewable energy' have emerged,
looking at how we can generate energy without burdening the earth or at least
by minimising the burden. Just look at the number of solar panels that have been
installed on commercial buildings in recent years.

I myself now also drive an electric car, and that immediately confronted me with
the sustainable facts; there is still a lot of work to be done around the electrification of vehicle fleets, both private and in and around commercial buildings.
Companies face numerous challenges: charging station infrastructure, providing
sufficient capacity, dismantling of car batteries, to name just a few. In this chapter,
we start a conversation about sustainability with Kristof Schrijvers. Kristof has

long worn two hats: one as a board member of IFMA Belgium and the other as the founder and managing partner of Green Jersey, an FM consultancy firm with a pronounced focus on sustainability. An ideal party to consult about the evolution of sustainability in general and in FM in particular.

A large part of this chapter is also dedicated to practical examples, approaching the subject from various angles. I am sure that at least one approach will align with your own reality. TU Delft teaches us how to deal with sustainability in various 'soft' topics, such as catering, for example. From FM Service Provider Facilicom, through their concept 'Buitengewoon', we learn how to focus on the social aspect and attempt to involve people who are distanced from the labour market. Furthermore, Edge Technologies explains how, as a real estate developer, technology can be involved to achieve sustainability. And at GraydonCreditsafe, I learn how they developed the 'ESG score' to map and clarify their own efforts and those of (external) partners. At Lenovo (Dubai), I highlight several very practical examples in their sustainability policy.

THE GROWING IMPORTANCE OF SUSTAINABILITY

Kristof Schrijvers

"SDG, ESG, CSRD, Scope 1, 2, 3... it's all about sustainability!" says Kristof Schrijvers commenting on the growing importance of sustainability. The more terms and acronyms that are coined for something, the greater its importance seems to be. In every company, in every sector, it's inescapable: you must and will conduct business with environmental awareness. In this context, people often speak of a green avalanche heading our way. And if we want to better understand how this avalanche was formed, says Kristof, we need to review some key moments from the past 50 years.

1972: publication of the book 'The Limits to Growth – A Report for the Club of Rome's Project on the Predicament of Mankind'. This is one of the first scientific reports, developed by the MIT (Massachusetts Institute of Technology) team, focusing on the exhaustion issues of our planet.

1987: presentation of the 'Brundtland Report'. This report, titled 'Our Common Future', stated that the major global environmental problems are the result of poverty and non-sustainable consumption and production. For the first time, it called for sustainable development, which they defined as meeting the needs of the present without compromising the ability of future generations to meet their own needs.

1997: the 'Kyoto Protocol'. With this treaty, industrialised countries agreed to reduce their greenhouse gas emissions, in the period between 2008 and 2012 (later extended to 2020), by an average of 5.2% compared to 1990 levels.

2000: the 'Millennium Development Goals' were established with the primary aim of eradicating global poverty. Eight concrete goals were laid out, which – unless stated otherwise – were to be achieved by 2015.

2015: the above goals were replaced by the 17 Sustainable Development Goals, better known as the SDGs. They were unanimously approved by all 193 countries of the United Nations and serve as a call to action to end poverty, protect the planet, and ensure prosperity for all. These goals focus on poverty eradication, climate action, clean energy, education, gender equality, and responsible consumption and production.

2015: UNFCCC – United Nations Framework Convention on Climate Change; this historical international treaty was agreed upon during COP21 (the 21st Conference of the Parties) of the UN climate agreement, with the aim of keeping the global average temperature increase well below 2°C compared to pre-industrial levels, and even aiming for a maximum increase of 1.5°C.

2018–2019: The Energy Performance of Buildings and Energy Efficiency Directives are revised within the framework of the 'Clean Energy for all Europeans Package' to meet the requirements set in the Paris Agreement but also to support the objectives of the upcoming Green Deal.

2019: Establishment of the Green Deal and announcement by the European Commission of a comprehensive plan to make Europe climate-neutral by 2050 and to make the economy more sustainable.

2020: As part of this plan, The Renovation Wave was launched, an initiative by the European Commission aimed at at least doubling the renovation rate of residential and non-residential buildings by 2030. Among other things, it states: "Two-thirds (65%) of the European building stock was built before 1980: about 97% of the EU's buildings must be upgraded to achieve the 2050 decarbonisation goal, but only 0.4–1.2% are renovated each year."*

End of 2022: The Corporate Sustainability Reporting Directive (CSRD) – the new European directive on sustainability reporting – came into effect. This directive obliges the 50,000 largest companies in Europe to report on the impact of their activities on people and the environment. The CSRD directive is central to the European Union's Green Deal and aims to provide more transparent and better sustainability information. In this way, the European Union intends to counteract greenwashing and direct resources towards truly sustainable companies. It forms an extension of the existing European directive on sustainability reporting, the Non-Financial Reporting Directive (NFRD), and will apply to all listed companies, public interest entities, and companies that meet the following criteria:

- More than 250 employees
- More than 40 million euros in turnover per year
- More than 20 million euros on the balance sheet

End of 2023: After the conclusion of COP28 – at the end of 2023, it should also be mentioned that at this meeting, for the first time, it was stated that fossil fuels will be phased out. This is a historic moment, but let us not be too quick to declare victory; much still needs to be done in this regard.

---

* https://www.bpie.eu

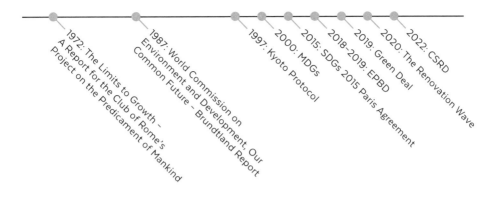

Figure 7.1: The ESG timeline.

WORK TO BE DONE ON SUSTAINABILITY

Quite a substantial list, right? And yet we must painfully conclude today that, despite all these pivotal moments and good intentions, the current transition is absolutely insufficient to reduce global warming to 1.5°C and to become CO_2 neutral by 2050. The Emissions Gap Report 2023[*] makes this very clear. This report states that globally we need to quickly transition to climate-neutral solutions. And this is precisely what the CSRD and associated legislation aim to achieve by requiring companies and their ecosystems to transparently disclose the steps being taken in this regard.

Every company, big or small, will need to have a sustainability strategy or will need to get to work on this quickly. When choosing suppliers or establishing partnerships, there will increasingly be inquiries about this strategy before potentially moving forward with a collaboration. But, as said before: it's better to start today than tomorrow. The chance increases day by day that even though you might not yet legally be required to report transparently on sustainability, you may be forced to do so by one of the companies from the ever-growing ecosystems with which you want to do business.

---

[*] https://www.unep.org/resources/emissions-gap-report-2023

TECHNOLOGY PAVES THE SUSTAINABLE WAY FOR THE EDGE

What's the best way to tackle this? Unfortunately, I cannot provide you with unequivocal, ready-made solutions. However, I can offer some excellent examples of how other companies have tackled this. Real estate developer The Edge in Amsterdam, for example, is regarded as a paragon of sustainable development in the facilities and workplace environment. Their approach to developing their new building, EDGE Stadium, might inspire anyone considering sustainable projects. The use of technology to achieve sustainability objectives is particularly striking. I discussed this with Ruud van der Sman, Head of Smart Solutions at Edge.

Ruud van der Sman

"Since building The Edge in Amsterdam, we have started developing blueprints for all aspects of construction and building management: safety, health, but also sustainability," Ruud says, "We always try to make the buildings energy-neutral, and technology plays a key role in this. This is also the case with the construction of EDGE Stadium in Amsterdam."

The use of data plays a key role in making the construction process and the buildings themselves sustainable, Ruud explains: "Data helps in planning cleaning, optimising energy consumption, and monitoring the well-being and health of employees. But they also help to make everything even more sustainable and to report according to ESG standards."

Another essential factor in using technology in FM is the cross-system and departmental approach, Ruud continues: "The silos need to be broken down. For example, motion sensors for lighting can be used for occupancy measurements or for security, and for optimal heating and ventilation."

This is also the case with the new building EDGE Stadium, says Ruud. Specifically: "The sensor in the lighting also measures temperature, how many people are present, humidity, sound, and light intensity. The sensor communicates wirelessly with other sensors nearby. All data are then sent to a central controller that then directs the operations for all techniques." Other technologies being used also promote sustainability. For instance, they use Visible Light Communication (VLC), data exchange via visible light, to let you know which room you are in at the office through an app on your smartphone. VLC is future-proof, not only because it has the potential to be much faster, but also because it is more energy-efficient than other communication technologies.

"Technology is an essential tool for making buildings sustainable, so you need to invest sufficiently in it," Ruud concludes. "The good news is that, if you implement technology correctly, from the start of the construction project, you also achieve maximum return and can better profile yourself as a leader in the sustainable real estate market." Asked about the quick wins, the technology that can be quickly integrated, Ruud points mainly to the different sensors: "so you know what is happening in your building and can respond to it".

TU DELFT: SUSTAINABILITY IN CONSTRUCTION AND SERVICES

How does sustainability find its way into all aspects of the world of FM, you wonder? To answer this question, I spoke with Andy van den Dobbelsteen, Sustainability Coordinator at TU Delft and also Professor in Climate Design & Sustainability. He was elected as CSR Manager of the year in the Netherlands in late 2023, and TU Delft is ranked 14th on the global sustainability list of universities.

Andy van den Dobbelsteen

By 2030, TU Delft aims to be fully CO_2-neutral, climate-adaptive, and circular, with a focus on quality of life and biodiversity. "Practise what you teach and preach. Climate change is progressing faster than predicted, so I set our sustainability goals for 2030, far enough off to initiate changes, close enough to feel the urgency," Andy explains. Calling him a shining example in sustainability is almost an understatement.

The university conducts a lot of research on sustainability and circularity, which has been used for over ten years to shape the university's policies. "Initially, we focused on energy use because everyone thought that was where the majority of emissions were located," says Andy, "but in 2019, we mapped out the entire emissions, revealing that it was almost entirely linked to three domains: travel, food, and natural gas consumption on campus (TU Delft purchases wind energy, so electricity use is formally CO_2-neutral). However, two years later, we gained insight into procurement – the purchase of furniture, equipment, office supplies, building materials, and other products – and its emissions turned out to be as significant as all other domains combined."

FM thus plays a significant role in their sustainability plans, but it is not limited to that department: "There is a high degree of community involvement: the entire campus community is involved, as well as external stakeholders. And there is a local sustainability coordinator for each faculty. They are required to develop their own plan based on our Vision, Ambition & Action Plan." This has already led to the replacement of natural gas with geothermal energy as a heat source and a revised food procurement policy, with much fewer animal products, as well as systematically including sustainability as a focal point in every tender.

More specifically on FM, this has led, among other things, to the construction of the Echo building, their latest educational building with various halls, used by all students and faculties. "We already had a building, Pulse, that is fully energy-neutral, but the Echo building produces more energy than it consumes," Andy proudly reports, "with a lot of wood and reusable structures for circularity".

The **catering services** are also fully committed to sustainability, offering vegetarian, mostly vegan restaurants instead of the traditional canteens. "We aim to transition to only 10% animal products," Andy adds, "Although there was external criticism, internal belief and acceptance on campus are strong. We've also received a lot of support from other campuses. The price is slightly higher than in traditional restaurants, but we're considering a CO2 weighting in food, making animal products more expensive than plant-based ones. At the coffee bars, cow's milk is already more expensive than oat, soy, almond, and coconut milk." Regarding **mobility**, Andy sees two ma-

jor changes: "On the one hand, we're working on a good arrangement for alternative solutions for commuting, making the ratio between car, public transport, and bicycles more sustainable. On the other hand, we want to minimise flying, and for business trips within 800 kilometres, taking a plane is no longer allowed."

As a Technical University, TU Delft naturally leads with its belief in and use of technology. Andy is confident they have the right researchers on campus for this: "We plan to test many innovations on campus, measuring everything to adjust as needed. For instance, we have a 24/7 lab with battery storage and hydrogen production. We store heat in the summer to use in the winter. Additionally, we're testing various new technologies, such as aquathermy, innovative solar techniques, and E-fuels, fuel made from CO_2, water, and electricity."

But they also look intensively at the past, especially at older buildings in need of renovation. Andy says, "Our real estate organisation mainly focuses on new construction, so renovation projects may have lower priority. However, this can be discussed as older buildings experience the greatest energy losses."

What lessons has Andy learned from the many sustainability initiatives in and around FM? "If I may give one piece of advice: start by thoroughly assessing your environmental impact. People are good at setting ambitions but often forget to measure and detail them. Look at all scopes, what directly or indirectly affects you, etc. As a business, you must be accountable for what you do. Therefore, you must also know the ecological impact of, for example, purchasing a computer. Practise what you preach and teach."

DISRUPTIVE WORKPLACES

FACILICOM: HOW CAN AN FM SERVICE PROVIDER ENSURE INCLUSION?

Sustainability is more than just environmentally conscious business, as demonstrated by FM Service Provider Facilicom. Their 'love for talent' extends beyond the ideal or even average employee, as evidenced by their inclusion policy. Within their walls, the social development company 'Buitengewoon' emerged in June 2018. "The main mission of this company is to guide people who experience a distance from the labour market to a job, through internships, work experience placements, and training," says Etienne Friederichs, initiator and (former) manager of Buitengewoon. "Initially, the company mainly focused on detachments within divisions of Facilicom Group, but now the talents are directly employed, and Buitengewoon supports the divisions in everything they need to maintain a sustainable workplace. We support between 70 and 80 people per year."

Etienne Friederichs

THE SOCIAL MISSION COMES BEFORE EVERYTHING.

The social mission certainly doesn't have to come at the expense of economic interests, even in an FM context, Etienne asserts: "Impact First: the social mission comes before everything. But if this is well organised, returns and growth will naturally follow, in our opinion. We combine our passion for people and entrepreneurship; we look at the people and what they need to work, and then try to find a place where this is possible. The appreciation we receive when we succeed is truly immense." Of course, economic interests also play a role, Etienne adds: "We also need to win new projects occasionally, but we feel that the urge to make a difference exists among our customers (the divisions of Facilicom Group) as well. And it doesn't have to be charity: if you do it right, it can be added value for everyone. Especially in large companies, the social impact in service provider contracts is a big advantage."

Etienne is also very optimistic about the future: "Companies like Buitengewoon have a distinct profile, which can make even more of a difference in the future. Additionally, today we see a huge shortage of talent on the one hand and a limited number of places where our talents can fit in on the other.

I expect that in the future, there will be much more focus on how to fill roles and tasks with these people as well." But he knows that the path to inclusive entrepreneurship is not always smooth, and it sometimes involves trial and error. But you shouldn't be discouraged by that, he adds: "If you really want this, then you have to do it. Choose an approach and adjust where necessary. And feel free to seek advice from stakeholders who have experience and are willing to share their knowledge."

Many companies and FM managers within these companies are by now convinced of the importance of ESG and, especially after reading this chapter, are eager to get started. But how do you know if you're on the right track? Can you quantify the results of your efforts? Can you get an ESG score for your company, like an Eco-score for your home or a Nutriscore for your food?

Since the IFMA event of 2023, I know that this ESG score exists. Graydon-Creditsafe's Head of ESG, Hind Salhane, explained this score then in a well-received keynote and later introduced me to the creator of this con-

Eric Van den Broele

cept, Eric Van den Broele, Director of Research & Development at GraydonCreditsafe. With him, we had a profound conversation about this ESG score and how companies should approach it best.

"The ESG score is a response to the many needs in the market regarding reporting and monitoring of how companies are dealing with ESG," Eric says. "On the one hand, you have mandatory reporting, as imposed by Europe since the Green Deal. On the other hand, you see that many aspects need to be brought together that historically have been far apart. Financial figures on the one hand, but also, for example, mapping behavioural patterns, such as stakeholder management, employee well-being, and environmental management in the hope that you can then predict them as well."

Traditionally, companies mainly have data on governance and sustainability; data on ecology were previously scarce, according to Eric: "This data is also not easy to capture. There are still no central databases collecting CO_2 emissions, logistical chains are not mapped out. You also need to pay attention to innovation capacity and efforts around circularity. Where you can already collect data more easily is (in the historical evolution of) the fleet. How does the percentage of electric cars and rail subscriptions grow, how many people come with (electric) bicycles, and do they receive a bicycle allowance? And how has this evolved in recent years?"

"The essence is also mainly in the fact that you can make deductions based on already known data. How do we measure innovation capacity? There is no direct measure for that. However, we now know from academic research that gender-diverse companies are more innovative. We also know that companies that are shock-resistant are more innovative. In addition, we can deduce from, for example, historical evolutions of the fleet or job vacancies whether there are signals from the company indicating attention towards the environment. Bring those elements together and you have a good chance of making a statement," Eric adds.

In total, 176 parameters are measured for all pillars combined: E, S, and G. By adding the correct weights to these, you arrive at a reliable overview. But what can you do with this score then? On the one hand, it serves as a measure for companies themselves to gauge their progress. On the other hand, it can be used externally as an argument to invest in them or to choose them as a supplier. Therefore, companies have every interest in scoring high here.

How do you then achieve the highest possible score? By working on it company-wide, Eric answers: "Every player in the company has a role to play in this. It's not just at the management level or a matter for FM and HR; all employees must be involved. Also, ensure that it remains a matter of 'wanting to' rather than 'having to'. If it's imposed, with a compliance manager and a top-down approach, it definitely won't work."

In any case, companies have a lot to think about, Eric explains: "You have to determine what social role you want and can play. You have to focus on inclusion. ESG should be part of every new project: the impact on the company, on the environment etc. But practical issues also need to be addressed, such as what budget you allocate for ESG initiatives. How can you achieve the greatest possible result with minimal effort? And where can the government participate in one of these scenarios?"

For the Facility Manager, it seems quite clear in which areas he or she can contribute, Eric suggests: "This relates to their specific services such as building management, fleet management, and energy management. But it can also involve seemingly minor details, such as the brand of coffee and whether it is sourced from fair trade. And the Facility Manager can also contribute in improving the well-being of employees, in consultation with the HR department, of course."

And that brings Eric to the first piece of practical advice for all Facility Managers: "You must not think in silos. The Facility Manager, like all colleagues, must break out of their silos and realise that ESG is a company-wide matter. Moreover, your suppliers and your internal collaboration should also be examined. As a Facility Manager, collaborate with external companies to see how you can join forces. And finally, link your ESG efforts to existing goals, so that everyone knows what you want to achieve and how."

THE IMPORTANCE OF FM IN ESG

What can you as a Facility Manager do concretely? As indicated in the introduction, we will all have to start reporting, and FM will play a central role in providing data for this. In chapter 2, we extensively highlighted how data management will form the basis for comprehensive business management in the future. Moreover, the use of AI (Artificial Intelligence) to make correct decisions will gain even more importance in the near future. IFMA has compiled a nice overview of the different domains you can utilise as an FM professional – see the next page. An important consideration here: develop your strategic plan with clear and SMART (Specific, Measurable, Achievable, Realistic, Time-bound) action points in the short, medium, and long term. The circle below can help determine your topics.

Beneficial certificates
For the building aspect of FM, there are also a plethora of certifications that represent sustainability, such as BREEAM, LEED, and WellBuild. What do these stand for again?
1. **BREEAM** stands for Building Research Establishment Environmental Assessment Method. It is a certification for achieving sustainable buildings and areas with minimal environmental impact.
2. **LEED** stands for Leadership in Energy and Environmental Design. It is a globally used standard for assessing ecological buildings.
3. The **WELL Building Standard** is an international standard for healthy buildings. It outlines specific criteria across 10 concepts: air, water, nourishment, light, movement, thermal comfort, acoustics, materials, mind, and community. Certain requirements are necessary to achieve the Well Building Standard certification.

Other important aspects in which the Facility Manager can contribute include certifications (see box). By obtaining these, you contribute to the branding of your company and the work environment you provide for your employees. When planning to relocate or renovate, be sure to consider these parameters and certifications during the design phase. Energy remains one of the parameters where quick wins can be achieved. Examine your energy consumption and associated contracts. Ensure you focus on sustainable energy; this is something you can expect from your current energy suppliers today. Additionally, in terms of fleet management, particularly through the electrification of the fleet, you can address a very hot topic.

Waste management may be a less obvious but equally important facet of ESG. Ensure that you use this as a selection criterion when choosing FM service providers: do the cleaning teams, for example, separate waste? Does your waste collector use smart containers to empty them centrally at the right times for recycling? If you have an onsite catering company, ensure they also have a sustainable waste policy and focus on food waste reduction. For coffee drinkers, alongside Fair Trade coffee, consider recyclable cups or porcelain mugs, where everyone is responsible for their own cup.

If you have green spaces, both internally and externally, ensure you also focus on biodiversity. Using greenery in the office enhances well-being and a comfortable feeling. Promoting biodiversity in green spaces in the external perimeter, on the other hand, benefits the environment; think of those much-needed bees. As previously mentioned, the entire workplace environment is crucial for focusing on well-being, and here too, technology can help with reporting. Chapters 2 and 4 extensively discuss how IoT and sensors can assist in this regard.

Especially involve external partners from your ecosystem in the search for sustainable opportunities. Specify requirements in the tendering process that specifically promote sustainability. This will only enhance collaboration in the future. Last but not least: provide a **business continuity plan** for your company. You can also contribute here: what if there is a flood, what if there is a blackout of energy supply, what if there is a cyber-attack? How will you ensure that people can keep working? Is there a temporary location where all facilities are up and running? We have just experienced a pandemic; how many companies have included a scenario in their plan for a future pandemic of that magnitude, or larger?

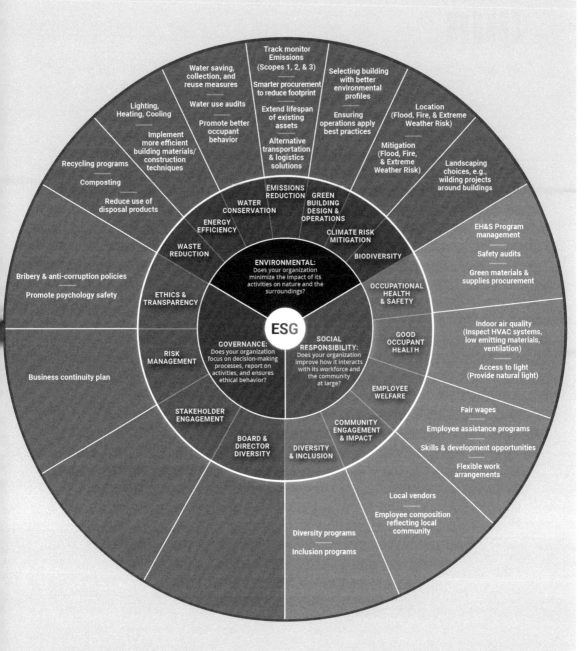

Figure 7.2 IFMA's ESG overview.

LENOVO

At Lenovo (Dubai), they have understood this well. Dhananjaya (Danu) Abesinghe, Regional Facility Manager, recently took thorough measures in managing the office in Dubai. Lenovo has a vision to achieve zero emissions by 2050.

- Workspaces: 100 for 220 employees, spread across two floors.
- Project timeline: December 2021 to September 2022

Dhananjaya Abesinghe

"The Dubai headquarters continues to focus on reducing waste, conserving energy and water, and providing model choices for sustainable facilities. We proudly announce that the Lenovo Dubai office no longer uses plastic bottles. We have refurbished 50 meeting rooms, chairs, and cabinets to save costs and resources. Our office water is the first worldwide in Lenovo to be reclaimed through humidity machines. As a result, we have achieved a 20% saving on our water bill. The plants we have selected in our office help reduce dust in the air, decrease carbon, stabilise moisture levels, and improve workplace well-being. Our cleaning materials are environmentally friendly and 100% sustainable. Electronic soap and paper towel dispensers reduce waste. 100% LED lighting throughout the office optimises indoor environmental quality.

This resulted in a 15% saving on the electricity bill. Additional sensors (temperature and occupancy) in the HVAC system optimise usage and minimise unnecessary electricity wastage. Waste materials from the office renovation project were minimised. We have recycled 100% of what we replaced, and

nothing has gone to landfill. We have shared our sustainable workplace performance with our employees. They love it," says Danu.

He adds, "We have also introduced wellness areas – with a pool table, Legion gaming zone, beautiful views, treadmills, distraction-free phone rooms, and focus rooms."

"WE HAVE SHARED OUR SUSTAINABLE WORKPLACE PERFORMANCE WITH OUR EMPLOYEES. THEY LOVE IT," SAYS DANU.

'THE ENTIRE WORKPLACE ENVIRONMENT IS CRUCIAL FOR FOCUSING ON WELL-BEING.'

7 STEPS TO SUCCESS

1. Identify your company's ESG strategy.
2. Determine the company's SDGs and apply them to FM and Workplace Experience, in the short, medium, and long term.
3. Manage the impact on your buildings.
4. Manage the impact on your services.
5. Manage the impact on DEI.
6. Explore how technology can assist.
7. Establish guidelines.

CHAPTER 8

THE FM SERVICE PROVIDER IN ALL ITS FACETS

During my student years, I had many holiday jobs: dishwasher in a large kitchen and distributing meals during lunch, waste collector in an office environment near a nuclear power plant, cleaner in a large warehouse in an industrial setting, warehouse worker, and loader and unloader of trucks etc. These diverse jobs have taught me that all these tasks in the FM sector are not only necessary but are also often damn hard work. Each of them forms an essential link in the facility process required to achieve quality service. Since then, I have immense respect for all the people who do their best to provide these services day in day out. For the majority of my career, I have been active with an FM Service Provider. This has led to a specific professional deformation: wherever I go, I check who is cleaning, which van is parked for maintenance, which company the security guards are from, and so on. It intrinsically interests me.

But it should actually interest everyone: The services of FM service providers contribute to the core process of your business. Try to imagine if they were absent and see what would happen then. If the receptionist were not there, who would greet visitors and ensure that the packages delivered to reception reached their destination? If the cleaning crew didn't come, how would you ensure clean toilets? How would you remove the coffee stains from the table in the meeting room where you are supposed to receive your clients in fifteen minutes? If the coffee machine were broken, who would provide that well-deserved coffee when you arrive at the office? If the HVAC (Heating Ventilation & Cooling) didn't work in the summer, how well could you concentrate in those sauna-like temperatures? Without all the facility services, you would undoubtedly experience lower productivity and employee satisfaction. So, you'd better think twice before questioning them.

In this chapter, the FM Service Provider gets all the attention. We discover how financial, health, and other crises impact budgets for FM services, and how FM service providers have responded with an agile approach. We learn about the current state of this market in Europe and the Middle East and how outsourcing models will evolve in the future. Last but not least, we travel through the region to talk to various leading FM service providers themselves about topics such as training, putting employees first, innovation, data-driven services, and much more. In conclusion, I provide advice on how to integrate all of this into your future-proof work environment.

FaaS (Facility as a Service) is the trendy name for flexible service provision by FM service providers and the accompanying outsourcing contracts. It seems like a new phenomenon, providing services based on changing situations and needs rather than rigid contracts with fixed hours and services. And it's true that FaaS is gaining traction due to budgetary pressures and changing working conditions: for example, it makes little sense to provide the same catering on Wednesdays and Thursdays when twice as many employees come to the office on Thursday. But the concept of flexible contracts and services is certainly not new; I myself have been advocating for it for over ten years. It's just that clients and service providers are much more open to it now. Roughly outlined, FaaS service providers have undergone the following evolution, from the perspective of contracts:

Figure 8.1: The different forms of contracts.

Resource-driven contracts: This could be described as 'hour-bound contracts': the calculation is made of how many hours are needed to provide certain services. For example, for a cleaning service, a supplier could – based on basic information provided by the client such as floor plans, a list of different types of spaces, flooring, and area – develop a cleaning programme and calculate the number of work hours required to accomplish it. This roughly determines the scope and cost of the contract.

Result-driven contracts: This type of contract first emerged fifteen years ago. A notable addition to these quotations and contracts was the concept of **'quality'**. Does this mean that in service provision with resource-driven contracts, there was no focus on quality? Absolutely not; these service providers also monitored quality during operational execution. However, at that time, quality was not used as a contractual condition or as a commercial argument, but rather controlled and not stipulated in the commercial or contractual process. For example, in our cleaning service, the client may not only provide the basic information mentioned above but also specify criteria regarding the quality expected for each space. The FM Service Provider can then decide how often and for how long they want to deploy their teams to achieve this result. In this context, the terms SLA (Service Level Agreement) and KPI (Key Performance Indicators) are often linked together.

Data-driven contracts: Meanwhile, we realise all too well that based on the above types of contracts, we cannot guarantee optimal service provision. Occupancy rates in office environments fluctuate greatly and this has a serious impact on the services required. Optimal service provision is only possible if we further expand the result-driven contract and exchange data between the client and FM Service Provider. Based on that data, service provision can better respond to the specific needs of that client. For example, our cleaning service will then add relevant data to its contract, such as the evolution of occupancy rates. If you know that Tuesdays and Thursdays are peak days for office presence, then you can adjust your cleaning programme and frequency accordingly and, of course, the same applies to days with lower occupancy, such as Wednesdays and Fridays. Catering can also be better utilised if it understands the peculiarities of the company. If we know that fewer people usually come to the office on Fridays, except for the first Friday of the month when happy hour is provided, then the caterer can better respond to the needs of each moment.

SHARING DATA: YOUR FM SERVICE PROVIDER AS A PARTNER IN EXCELLENCE

From the above list of contract types, you can already deduce that sharing data is becoming an integral part of quality service delivery. Almost naturally, this leads to more of a partnership model rather than a standard customer-supplier model. Your FM service provider becomes a 'partner in excellence', so to speak. If you are a catering provider for a company with a headquarters employing 1,000 people, you would like to gain insight into the number of individuals present in the building per day. The client has this information, either through the badge system or through a workplace reservation system (IWMS). If the client shares this data with you, as an FM Service Provider, you can tailor your catering offerings accordingly. This, in turn, has a positive impact on sustainability and effective waste management; of course, you could provide food every day for a much higher number of end customers, never taking risks, but nobody benefits from such food waste.

The so-called 'Hard Service' FM service providers, on the other hand, benefit from data from the BMS (Building Management System). This allows them to evolve their maintenance from curative and preventive to prescriptive. This means they no longer schedule maintenance when something is broken or well in advance, but rather base their maintenance on data collected on various parameters such as comfort, cost, and energy. An automatic workflow can then be set up to perform maintenance. In Gartner terminology, this is also referred to as 'Hyperautomation'. However, this can only happen if there is a good relationship between the customer and the supplier, and if there are clear agreements regarding the provision of that data. So, both parties need to act as partners.

WHAT OUTSOURCING MODEL IS IDEAL FOR YOU NOW?

Armed with our knowledge of various contract forms, we can enter the service market, exploring what is being offered. But it's best not to do so unprepared.

Always start by asking yourself what you want to do yourself and **what you will outsource**. The rule of thumb here, for me and many others, is: If it's not part of your core processes, you're better off outsourcing it, so you have more time to focus on what you strategically invest in and where you can make a difference. And only for a minority of companies do facility services belong to those core tasks. In that case, it's better to outsource those services to FM service providers, for whom this is part of their core activities. FM services often involve complex processes that deserve attention.

This specialisation has led to a common principle in the FM service sector: the TUPE (Transfer of Undertakings Protection of Employment) principle. This principle aims to protect employees when a service contract moves from one provider to another; often, employees are also transferred to the new service provider. This is a very common procedure among providers of cleaning, catering, and security services. But it also often happens during a transition of employees from the client to the FM Service Provider.

Another question is, of course, **which levels** you wish to outsource: operational, tactical, and/or strategic? Opinions on this vary considerably. My view on this is that as a company, you should always keep a portion of the strategy in your own hands. This way, you can set your own course and survey the market to develop the ideal outsourcing model to achieve your facility objectives. These objectives depend on where FM is positioned within your company. If we frame this in a very black-and-white context, finance focuses on cost awareness and functional services, HR focuses on well-being and employee experience, real estate focuses on the balance between square metres used and the and services tailored to them. These are just a few examples. As I preached earlier, ensure that FM is discussed at the strategic level so that you can contribute to company-wide challenges such as hybrid working, the employee journey, employee retention, real estate policy, etc.

Below, we provide a visual overview of the outsourcing models available and how they can be linked to the various levels of outsourcing from operational to strategic.

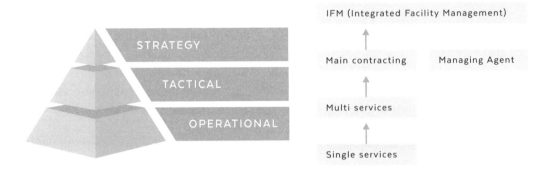

Figure 8.2: outsourcing models.

In '**Single Services**', you enter into individual contracts with various FM service providers. You contract specialists yourself for each different domain. In this case, you assume that you have strong FM in-house and can manage all of this yourself. A next level of outsourcing is '**Multi Services**'. Bundling different services with the same FM Service Provider, who can perform all these services. Here, you can work with an SPOC (Single Point of Contact) principle: one contact person at your FM Service Provider for these different services. This makes it somewhat simpler for management and follow-up.

Moving up another level, we talk about '**main contracting**'. Here, you combine a multi-services contract with an FM Service Provider with some single services from other parties, which you have sought out yourself but which are included under the multi-services contract. Think of services like green maintenance, elevator maintenance, pest control, etc. The complexity of such an outsourcing model can increase significantly, and often the FM Service Provider will deploy a 'Facility Coordinator' or 'Facility Manager' in such contracts to manage everything for you. The tactical and strategic management still remains in your hands as the client. In this outsourcing model, we often see '**managing agents**' emerging, FM service providers that focus solely on management and offer few or no executive services. This can be a solution if the client lacks the internal resources to manage all FM services.

Finally, we arrive at **IFM** (Integrated FM), the pinnacle of outsourcing: all services are placed under one FM Service Provider, who also takes care of tactical management and follow-up. In the past, it was often suggested that this is the path to take and that everyone should adopt this concept. However, every company is unique, so it's best to first check how your organisation and FM operate before determining your outsourcing model. Perhaps the number of service providers is limited enough to keep everything in-house. Or maybe you have a strong FM team that can manage this better than any service provider? In any case, I recommend keeping strategic oversight as a client in-house.

Finally, the above picture is obviously a simplified representation, and there are still many variations and intermediate models possible. I mainly wanted to provide a general overview. But for those who want to delve further into all the possibilities, feel free to reach out to me.

THE EMEA MARKET OF FM SERVICE PROVIDERS IN A NUTSHELL

What does the market of FM service providers actually look like? Is this a market to take into account on a global economic scale? Well, judge for yourself. The following figures and table, for which I thank research firm Frost & Sullivan, provide you with an idea of the size and evolution of this market.

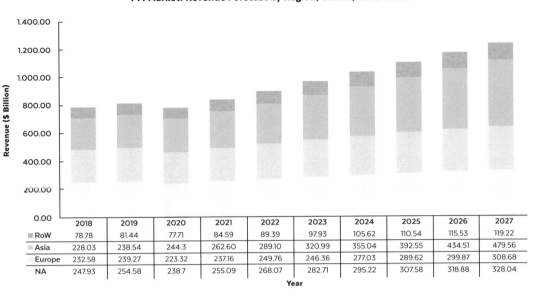

FM Market: Revenue Forecast by Region, Global, 2018-2027

	2018	2019	2020	2021	2022	2023	2024	2025	2026	2027
RoW	78.78	81.44	77.71	84.59	89.39	97.93	105.62	110.54	115.53	119.22
Asia	228.03	238.54	244.3	262.60	289.10	320.99	355.04	392.55	434.51	479.56
Europe	232.58	239.27	223.32	237.16	249.76	246.36	277.03	289.62	299.87	308.68
NA	247.93	254.58	238.7	255.09	268.07	282.71	295.22	307.58	318.88	328.04

Figure 8.3: Overview global evolution of the FM service providers market – Frost & Sullivan.

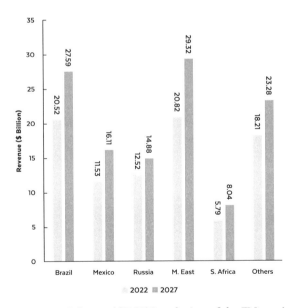

Figure 8.4: Overview 'rest of the world ROW' evolution of the FM service providers market – Frost & Sullivan.

From this overview, it appears, among other things, that the total market amounts to over 1 trillion (1,000 billion) dollars in 2024, and that we can expect growth of at least 10% by 2027. Europe accounts for approximately a quarter of this market, and the Middle East about 2.5%. Notably, integrated facilities management (IFM) services are growing much stronger than 'single' and 'bundled services', but for now, single services still dominate, as you can see in the figure below.

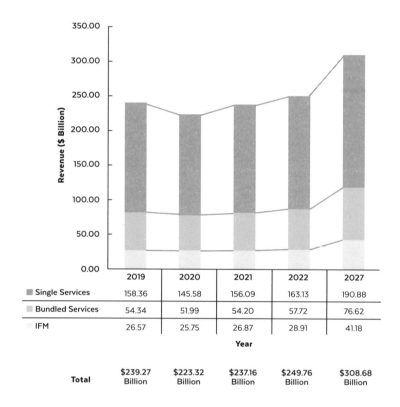

	2019	2020	2021	2022	2027
Single Services	158.36	145.58	156.09	163.13	190.88
Bundled Services	54.34	51.99	54.20	57.72	76.62
IFM	26.57	25.75	26.87	28.91	41.18
Total	$239.27 Billion	$223.32 Billion	$237.16 Billion	$249.76 Billion	$308.68 Billion

Figure 8.5: Overview of total FM market by contract type Europe – Frost & Sullivan.

TRENDS IN THE FM SERVICE PROVIDERS MARKET

Frost & Sullivan remains a valuable source of information when discussing this FM services market. Not only do they continuously collect data, but they are also very active in identifying old and new trends in this market. I have always found their reports and analyses very valuable, which is why I engaged in a conversation with one of their partners, John Raspin.

John Raspin

In general, you can observe an **upward trend in the value chain**. John opens his argument, saying: "It's becoming increasingly difficult for service providers to differentiate themselves, and at the same time, you see that customers are becoming increasingly aware of what they want. Therefore, service providers want to profile themselves less as price fighters and more as partners with added value. They want to become advisors to the customer and offer solutions that address their specific needs." The demand for advice to improve the workplace has increased tremendously due to the Covid pandemic as a major disruptor: "Suddenly, everyone woke up and realised what was possible with the right FM services. Many use cases that had been lying around for a long time could suddenly be implemented more quickly."

The importance of **ESG** (Environmental, Social, Governance) has also increased enormously for FM service providers in recent years. John notes: "Customers have put this higher on the agenda, and therefore expect it from service providers. These service providers are happy to comply because it not only positions them competitively but also allows them to save costs themselves." The importance of technology in this cannot be overstated, according to John: "Many companies have clear objectives but may not immediately know how to measure them. FM service providers who use the right technology can greatly assist their clients and prove their added value. However, this is often easier for small service providers than for large ones because they can respond more quickly to new trends and innovations."

The impact of Covid is particularly noticeable in the area of **hybrid work environments**, John continues: "Customers no longer have a choice; they must enable the hybrid work environment. No one can compel all employees to come to the office every day anymore, and especially for routine tasks, employees usually stay at home. For employers, the challenge is no longer providing enough space, but rather making the office spaces attractive so that employees feel like coming instead of feeling obligated. If you don't do that, they'll go elsewhere. That's why FM service delivery needs to change, and so do service providers. FM providers who continue to anchor their business model to the number of square metres will find it very difficult."

The advent of more **data and digital tools** also has significant implications for FM service providers, John explains: "It started with the use of sensors and analytics to achieve more efficient service delivery through resource and planning optimisation. Now, savvy companies are leveraging innovation for new types of services, such as predictive services and remote services. They can engage with customers at a whole new level." For instance, 'workplace apps' to support employees at their workplace are popping up like mushrooms, whereas not long ago, nobody knew what such an app was. Regarding the advanced deployment of AI and robotics, John believes it will take a bit longer: "Indeed, this could greatly alleviate human work, but I expect it will take another five to ten years before it truly takes off. Today, some service providers use it to automate processes, and we already see cleaning or gardening robots appearing here and there, but we're still largely in the exploration phase."

Finally, John emphasises the importance of the end-user in the evolution of FM service providers: "Previously, the employer was your customer, and you only needed to keep them satisfied. Today, the employee experience is crucial in what you do. They are the end-users, but they are also influencers, whom you'd better keep satisfied. That's a radically different approach compared to before." At the same time, you still need to maintain a good balance between innovation and pragmatism – the customer still expects cost savings – and always consider the maturity of your customer. It's a delicate balance, that's for sure.

A JOURNEY THROUGH THE REGION – MEET SOME STRIKING FM SERVICE PROVIDERS

After the figures and trends, it's high time to let FM service providers speak for themselves. For this purpose, we travel across Europe and the Middle East to achieve the broadest possible overview. At the same time, we shed light on as many aspects as possible of the everyday reality for these service providers. This way, you also get a comprehensive overview of the broad range of activities of FM service providers, where they stand today, and how this market will evolve in the coming years.

Tariq Chauhan

EFS, internationally active in Africa, the Middle East, Asia, and Europe, with headquarters in Dubai, employs around 22,000 people. One of their biggest challenges is to sustain growth and international presence by attracting more and more new talent. Not easy with a job market where a significant gap exists between school education and the reality of working for an FM service provider, notes Tariq Chauhan, Group CEO & Co-Founder of EFS: "That's why we invest in so-called 'incubation centres,' nine-month training programmes for young leadership potential, preparing them for the job they will have to perform. In recent years, 500 new talents have graduated from here." A significant part of the training is on-the-job training, adds Tariq: "There are too few experienced people available, so they need training on the job. But for that, we have to rely on the flexibility of our clients."

Recruiting and retaining talent is crucial for EFS, and therefore the company continues to heavily invest in training for current employees: "The ROI of this, retaining your talent, is enormous when you consider that employees make up 70% of our costs, and retaining an employee is always cheaper than having to replace someone. Not only because of recruitment costs but also because experienced employees are usually more productive. And – last but not least – it fits with our 'people first' philosophy that every employee is important. They are our ambassadors, and we do everything to make that ambassador shine."

Jan Dunkelberg

Apleona Group, a German FM service provider with around 40,000 employees active across Europe, Africa, and the Middle East, also faces challenges in filling all necessary skills, CSO Jan Dunkelberg tells us: "Workplace management is a relatively new topic for FM service providers, or combatting sustainability and reducing carbon emissions through digitalisation. Questions like 'How can we actively measure and report our ecological efforts with available technology?' or 'How do we integrate this into the IFM contracts?' scream for new talent, people who have mastered all of this, and you don't always find them internally. New jobs are emerging for us that combine environmental and sustainability concerns with the new expectations around workplace management. And people who can use AI for predictive maintenance. Filling all these new vacancies is not easy."

Another challenge Jan sees is getting employees back to the office: "Especially in the United Kingdom, we are focusing hard on this. We are researching intensively what is needed to convince people. For example, the food in the canteen can play a big role. Serving healthy food can be very important in this campaign to get people back to the office."

CLOUDFM - A CULTURE OF TRANSPARENCY AND TRUST

Jeff Dewing, CEO of Cloudfm, wrote a book titled 'Doing the Opposite.' That immediately caught my attention: How would this British FM service provider do the opposite of others? I spoke with him and received the following response: "We are a fairly young company and because of that, we were able to do several things completely differently from others. One of the fundamental differences is that we started from technology instead of trying to integrate it afterwards like most established entities. This led to interesting new approaches. For example, the technology to manage all activity across all clients was built to work completely differently from the established market. In all comparable technologies, you can edit, manipulate, and delete data, but not with this software. The result is that you may not always like the data, but you know it's the truth."

Another example is IoT, Jeff continues: "Instead of sticking thousands of sensors on devices, we designed and built a 'smart box' to be placed in an electrical distribution panel, which powers the assets. This smart box monitors both energy and harmonics and provides much more data than all sensors combined ever could. And those are just a few examples."

Jeff Dewing

Despite or, according to Jeff, perhaps thanks to this focus on technology, Cloudfm pays remarkable attention to corporate culture, both within the company itself and with customers: "When you serve a small number of large clients and establish a sustainable relationship with them, this also impacts your employees: they feel safe and secure and know that they are allowed to make mistakes in their pursuit of creativity. We adapt ourselves to the customer but also the customer to us. But above all, our partnerships are based on core values, made possible by technology, such as transparency, collaboration, and trust. Together, we embark on a journey towards the best possible FM collaboration." This culture of transparency and trust also applies to our own employees: "They can work from home seamlessly if circumstances allow, as long as they carry out their assigned tasks according to our agreement."

COOR – DATA-DRIVEN SERVICES

Coor is one of the leading FM service providers in the Nordics (Sweden, Norway, Denmark, and Finland), claiming to hold a 40% market share in the IFM segment. Their 13,000 employees are predominantly active in Northern Europe, fostering a personal connection to better understand and cater to their clients' needs. This results in close collaborations with major companies and some notable partnerships. For instance, Coor is responsible for maintaining the well-known bridge between Sweden and Denmark.

But according to Erik Sörnäs, Deputy Senior Vice President of Business Development at Coor Group, the close relationship and sense of familiarity are not the only success factors for Coor. He says, "Our services are increasingly data-driven, utilising data from sensors and other indicators to monitor and ultimately improve our services. Predictive maintenance, ensuring maintenance and replacements are done when truly needed and not too early or too late, was until recently merely a topic of discussion, but today, it is our reality."

Erik Sörnäs

To leverage the right data, it is also crucial to collaborate with the client, Erik learned. "It must be a real win-win for both parties, with common goals and ambitions, and with clear agreements, just like in any marriage." This innovative approach also leads to a new type of contracts: "Traditional criteria such as cost and SLAs with associated penalty systems are replaced by a culture of collaboration and creating added value." This added value primarily lies in the employee experience. Therefore, Coor has developed a comprehensive app called Simply by Coor, allowing users to reserve parking spaces, sign up for yoga classes, check the catering menu, and more. Sustainability is also not forgotten in their data strategy. With their carbon assessment tool, they can measure their clients' ecological footprint in various areas (water, commuting, energy consumption, etc.) to use this data as a basis for environmentally-friendly initiatives.

eFM - EMBRACING TECHNOLOGY (PARTNERS)

eFM (Etisalat FM), operating in the Middle East and Africa with approximately 3,500 employees, is a part of Etisalat Telecom, both based in the United Arab Emirates. It was one of the first FM providers to offer energy management as a service, with a contract based on profit sharing. The model was highly successful, attracting clients such as Dubai Police and Abu Dhabi Airport.

For over a decade, Etisalat has been collaborating with technology partners, says Ibrahim Moursy, Senior Director of Business Development & Growth at eFM. "For our security service, we have partnerships with suppliers of CCTV cameras, behaviour recognition software, AI, and other technologies supporting our department. This isn't a luxury because even with over 1,000 security guards, we still needed more hands."

Ibrahim Moursy

And the innovation story doesn't end there. Technology also makes a difference for operational teams. They have recently started using Augmented Reality for better maintenance: technicians on-site are connected with a specialist at the office, and through their AR glasses, the specialist can provide advice and training remotely. "This optimises our resources, facilitates knowledge sharing, and it's even cheaper," Ibrahim explains. He also highlights the use of cleaning robots with a docking station for thorough daily cleaning in a shopping centre after hours: "The robot is programmed according to the maintenance schedule, and the result is fantastic. We've freed up four cleaners who no longer need to push machines and can focus on tasks with higher added value, while the robots perform repetitive tasks better than anyone else, consistently delivering high quality."

SODEXO – ELEVATING FM TO A STRATEGIC LEVEL

Henrik Jarleskog

With Henrik Jarleskog, Regional Head of Strategy at Sodexo, I like to delve into the strategy of this global player in the FM services market, with a staggering 422,000 employees worldwide. "As an FM service provider, you obviously need a global strategy," he responds, "but at the same time, you also need to ensure a strategy per region and even per country. You need to understand the macroeconomic trends in the labour market as well as sense the differences within and between regions. Each country has its own culture and legislation, and it's important to find a 'fit' with them." And this focus on strategy is certainly not superfluous because more and more companies have elevated FM to a strategic level: "The workplace is now on the agenda during boardroom meetings, and the operational model for FM can play a role here. So, we also need to be able to talk to them at that strategic level."

One of the key concepts in these discussions is hybrid working, says Henrik: "You can no longer contract based solely on occupancy rates; you must adapt to the ever-changing reality and demonstrate great flexibility. However, agility is far from easy due to the lack of a clear legal framework in many countries." Yet some principles remain unchanged: "You must base decisions on employee experience rather than any preferences of the management team. And you must adopt a sustainable and inclusive policy."

To achieve sustainability, Sodexo also heavily relies on technology: "Digital twins of buildings are highly relevant if you have enough sensors and data available. You can truly impact energy consumption when you gain better insight into usage patterns and can optimise services accordingly." Sodexo is already fully embracing this approach, and they know why: "Sustainability and ecological awareness are here to stay. Governments are imposing more and more requirements in these areas. So, it's better to take action now and reap the economic benefits immediately."

VEBEGO – PUTTING EMPLOYEES AT THE CENTRE AND IN THE SPOTLIGHT

Mark van Haasteren

Vebego, headquartered in the Netherlands, is a well-known player in Belgium, the Netherlands, Germany, and Switzerland, with approximately 21,000 employees. I also spoke with their Chief Operational Officer, Mark van Haasteren, about the evolutions in the FM services market and Vebego's strategy for it.

Mark starts on a positive note: "FM services such as hygiene and cleaning have come to the forefront. Previously, this was always done outside office hours, but today, it's becoming increasingly visible how important these services and the people who provide them are. This has had an impact on FM in general and our strategy in particular." Vebego still sees many competitors focusing on price and volume, but precisely because of the increased attention to FM at a strategic level, Vebego opted for the opposite approach: "We put our people at the centre and in the spotlight. We try to have them work as much as possible during office hours. And we select our clients based on this; if they only care about price, we'd rather not work with them.

We want to stay away from being seen as a commodity and instead provide more added value, including a focus on hospitality." This way, Vebego also hopes to be a more attractive employer in this tight labour market. However, the company is also convinced that there are opportunities in attracting people who are distant from the labour market.

And what about technology? Does Vebego heavily invest in AI, IoT, and robotics? "We closely monitor the possibilities and have already launched some use cases, but there is a lot of hype in this sector. Besides, at Vebego, we've had the best sensors in the world for many years: our people, who go everywhere and see everything!"

SELECTING FM SERVICE PROVIDERS: A GUIDE

Are you now convinced that you also need (more) external FM service providers? Below is a step-by-step plan and some points to consider. You should start with your '**as is**' situation. What and how do you outsource, and what do you still do yourself? Do the contract forms still meet the current way of working, and how are your outsourcing models? Once you have mapped all of this, look at the role FM plays at the company level and its impact within your organisation. What does it contribute to? It's important to consult various **stakeholders**, as discussed in chapter 5, and involve them in painting a clear picture of where the company wants to go. You need to have this mapped out clearly before you start surveying the market. You can delve quite deep and wide into this:

- What do the employees in your company expect from service provision?
- What do your management and board expect? The importance they attach to FM and the workplace will determine the budget you will have available to spend on FM service providers. An important consideration they can (and actually should) take into account is: How can all of this contribute to company branding? What is the impact of a 'wow' effect on visitors and job applicants when they enter your company, and how much is that impact worth to you?
- Colleagues from other departments are usually involved parties as well. Finance wants to know what investments are needed and what return they can expect. ICT wants to know what technology is needed, whether integration needs to be made with existing systems, what goes into the cloud, and – last but not least – how cybersecurity is addressed. With HR, you examine outsourcing from the perspective of how it will contribute to the company's strategic workplace policy as part of 'employer branding'. And the real estate department wants to be able to integrate this with overall building management and associated aspects such as lease contracts.

These are just a few examples of how crucial stakeholder management is to get a good overview of your 'as is' and what you could potentially become. And how is FM and the workplace viewed within your company? Is it seen as a cost or as added value? Depending on how you shift on this axis, you may be able to tender more appealing matters and make your workplace a pleasant meeting space. The more strategically you can deploy FM in the workplace, the better for your available budget.

Other factors that also play an important role in your selection of FM service providers:

- Are you active only **nationally** or also **internationally**? This partly determines whether you prefer a local, regional, or global FM service provider. Look at how the players operate where your company is located, check their strong references, and see if they're a match for your company. A regional or global player isn't always equally strong in every country they operate in, so don't let their international reputation sway you too much.
- What should you definitely include in your **SLAs** & **KPIs** beyond standard items like quality service, processes, communication and reporting, and financial reporting? What makes your company unique and how can an FM service provider contribute to that uniqueness? Suppose your company operates in software; is your future FM service provider also engaged in deploying technology and innovation? That could be an ideal match.
- Several things should not be overlooked when selecting and negotiating with a service provider. ESG reporting, for instance: what do you want to focus on and what do you want to monitor for this? But innovation will also be a significant factor in future service delivery; you need to ensure the FM service provider remains alert and comes up with proposals at least once a year to optimise service delivery. You're aided by a constantly changing market; this provides plenty of opportunities to inquire how they'll deal with these changes. And, relentlessly: data, data, data. Clearly define who provides what data and make contracts flexible and dependent on available data.
- The entire spectrum that can contribute to your needs should be examined. How does your FM service provider focus on **hospitality** and how does that contribute to the employee experience? Consider how you can also involve sustainability and work with local parties for services such as concierge services: ironing, fruit delivery, car washing in the company parking lot etc. Create an employee journey for your own company, map it out, and work with a 'star' system like in the hotel sector: How many stars of service do I want and can I offer to my colleagues? Imagine a reception service where hospitality staff walks up to greet you, where

you're pre-registered so the receptionist knows immediately who you have an appointment with, where you've received clear email instructions in advance on how to reach the parking area, with a code for guest Wi-Fi, and so on, where you're immediately offered something to drink and can wait in a comfortable lounge until your host comes to pick you up. How many stars would you give such a reception, and how much are you willing to invest to offer that to your guests?

■ Never underestimate the importance of **feedback**. Ensure you continuously monitor and follow up on the experience of employees, your users of FM services. This provides invaluable data if you wish to re-enter the market. You can learn a lot from this. You can use an annual digital survey, but also satisfaction surveys throughout the building. For example, you can display a QR code on a screen in the restaurant to evaluate how satisfied they were with the meal, the service, the waiting times, and other interesting feedback. This is very useful information and can also be used in the operational phase of your contracts by linking them to SLAs and KPIs. Make sure you also establish a feedback group with various stakeholders with whom you engage in conversation several times a year to gauge their opinions on the current service provision. Ask them what could be improved, how they would solve it, etc.

■ Create an ideal scenario of your '**to be**' situation. Provide a clear description ('Specifications of Work') for all the services you want to inquire about. Incorporate the above points to make your description complete. Make it clear to the market what the hard requirements are and what the 'nice to haves' are.

■ Then go to the market and enquire with different FM service providers. Consider this your market exploration. As a result, you'll be able to further align your 'to be' with reality. Then, in collaboration with the purchasing team, it's time to initiate your purchasing process. Pay particular attention to the cost/quality ratio in your evaluation. The cheapest solution is usually not the right one!

SOME CLOSING THOUGHTS

Education from both sides

It came up regularly during our journey through the FM service provider landscape: FM is a people business, with individuals who also value a good work-life balance. Traditionally, cleaning activities are done early in the morning (6am–9am) or late in the evening (5pm–8pm). Why couldn't this just be done during office hours? Many of these tasks are non-disruptive and can easily be carried out. This often contributes to a better perception of the service when employees see the cleaning crew present and the tasks they are performing.

Legislation supports the agile approach

Everyone is seeking more agile services, both the client and the supplier. But for this to happen, government and legislation need to evolve as well. In many countries, collective labour agreements are in place, with requirements regarding the minimum number of hours an employee is deployed or restrictions on performing specific tasks in certain sectors. For example, a catering staff member may not always be able to assist the cleaning crew, or a hospitality worker may not be able to work with the catering team. My call to legislators: make this flexible, ensure that with the limited resources available, we can still carry out necessary tasks within clear and simple legislation that enables agile contract forms.

Cost savings – are they still possible?

The largest wave of cost savings in FM and workplace management occurred in 2008 and the subsequent years (the years of the financial crisis). Back then, it was common to set up contracts with required savings over three or five years, for example, 5% savings after one year, 3% after two, 2% after four, and so on. The general feeling among both FM service providers and FM professionals within companies, like myself, is that there isn't much left to cut. All logical savings have already been identified and implemented. In my opinion, we've reached a tipping point where the primary driver shouldn't be cost savings but optimisation across various domains, which would ultimately lead to cost savings again but is no longer the main goal. Technology plays a significant role here.

Investments in technology as partners

Contracts with FM service providers are usually concluded for three to five years. This makes it challenging for suppliers to heavily invest in technology. That's why I propose a collaborative approach, where you collectively explore how to focus on optimisations in daily operational execution. Cobots or robots could play a significant role here. If they can take over routine tasks, it could allow employees to take on other facility-related tasks. IoT sensors or QR codes can also contribute to this, as we learned from the various portraits of FM service providers. As you can see, setting up the ideal FM service is more complex than one might initially think. But with this chapter, you already have some inspiration and practical tips to take those first steps towards your future-oriented workplace!

7 STEPS TO SUCCESS

1. In what form of outsourcing contracts are you currently engaged?
2. Determine your data sharing policy.
3. Align your outsourcing model with your organisation.
4. Compile a list of potential FM service providers in your region.
5. Review upcoming trends and relate them to your organisation.
6. Create an 'as is' snapshot.
7. Define your 'to be' ideal situation and survey the market.

CHAPTER 9

GEN Z : NOT A CONCERN BUT A BLESSING

"T hings used to be better." That's what our grandparents used to say to our parents, which our parents repeated to us, and in a moment of vulnerability, I too sometimes find myself thinking the same. But I'm sober enough to realise that this has more to do with a changing world than with the qualities of those successive generations.

I myself hover somewhere between the end of Generation X and the beginning of Generation Y, seeing aspects of both generations reflected in myself. However, with my children, you'll find a straight-up Gen Z-er (Birthe) and a Gen Alpha (Bent). Without delving into what characterises each generation, there's one striking common factor: their relationship with technology is vastly different from mine. I might even dare to call them 'Smombies', you know, that fusion of 'smartphone' and 'zombie'. The smartphone seems to be glued to their hands, and all too often, the world around them is almost non-existent. It's no coincidence that many schools are implementing bans on smartphones: only then can you expect even the slightest attention from this generation of youth, or so it seems.

The attention given to the small screen and the social media accessed through it is less extreme among those in their thirties and forties, but I still catch myself spending a lot of time on social media. Following media and influencers on YouTube, Instagram, and other TikToks has become commonplace. And the day when social media, and by extension the entire digital world, play a significant role in our work experience is probably not far off. We already see companies using influencers to advertise certain clothing and food brands. So why wouldn't digitalisation extend to FM and our workplace? I can already envision us soon spending time with our avatars in a digital office environment in Roblox or Fortnite. Perhaps we'll even have an office in 'the Metaverse' one day? Such changes will occur much faster as the next, more digital generations enter the workforce.

When I started working in 2004, we experienced something similar; our – then still truly young – generation was much more adept with computers and new technology than the older generations at the time. We were fully on board with the (r)evolution of the internet and mobile devices, eagerly embracing it and immediately applying its many benefits in our daily work. For the older generation, it all took a bit longer. Granted, the above description is somewhat generalised: there are also technology enthusiasts among the older generation and young people who prefer to stay away from social platforms. But I am convinced that as Facility Managers, we can contribute to an environment where all generations feel at home and can interact with each other. And in this chapter, we will explore exactly how this can be achieved.

To do this, we start with a brief description of the different generations, their characteristics, and the differences between them. Then we visit Breda University of Applied Sciences to talk to some Gen Z-ers about how they perceive the workplace. I also briefly touched base with Gen Z-ers who have just entered the workforce. Of course, this is not a large-scale study, but it gives you an idea of how we should further evolve the workplace. Leadership plays a significant role here. The Chair of IFMA Belgium Chapter, Nathalie Cloet, Senior Facility Manager at Beckton Dickinson (BD), introduced me to their 'Next Gen' project team, who was keen to share some practical examples with us. Finally, I would like to explain which parameters we need to consider to shape a sustainable, future-proof work environment.

WHO ARE THE GENERATIONS IN THE WORKPLACE TODAY?

To ensure clarity, I'll provide an overview of the different generations currently active in the labour market. The exact start and end dates of each generation may vary depending on the source, but these differences typically don't result in significant discrepancies. To pre-empt any debates or concerns, I'd like to mention that the following information regarding years and descriptions is based on the insightful book 'Generation Zalpha: connecting with the Next Micro-Generation' by author Maarten Leyts.

Baby Boomers (1946 – 1964): This is the generation of my parents, most of whom have since retired. Their focus was primarily on job security, and their careers were characterised by long tenures with the same employer. They adhered to the 'management by presence' principle, typically working in a '9-to-5' routine. A majority of this generation struggled with the rapid evolution of technology, social media, and various communication channels. They were strongly oriented towards hard work. This generation began their careers without technology in the workplace, and the advent of digitalisation forced them to catch up. For them, technology is a 'tool', a means to an end.

Generation X (1965 – 1979): This generation was the first to experience digitalisation in the office. Each office worker had their own space with a PC (back then, we didn't yet refer to them as desktops) and a telephone. Over time, the internet, laptops, and mobile phones also made their entrance, and everyone learned to communicate via email and SMS. This generation also questioned the 9-to-5 mentality, introducing 'management by results'. The introduction of flexible working hours in the workplace provided more flexibility, further enhanced by the option of remote work. Gen X is the generation that aims for a better work-life balance but also possesses a strong work ethic, likely influenced by observing both parents working hard during their youth.

Generation Y / Millennials (1980 – 1994): This generation increasingly values freedom and flexibility, supported by the digital world they grew up in. The introduction of tablets and smartphones allowed them to be reachable and work from anywhere. The workplace gained an extra dimension, enabling work from home, satellite offices, on the go, or at a client's site. The rise of social media also fostered extensive digital connectivity. Everyone is constantly reachable, sometimes leading to excessive multitasking – social interaction permeates everything they do – but also to FOMO (Fear Of Missing Out) and the feeling of the constant necessity to be available. They no longer see technology as a tool but as an extension of their personality. They are always focused on personal growth.

Gen Z (1995 – 2009): This generation is currently taking their first steps into the job market. They are true 'digital natives', and contemporary technology – Metaverse, AI, TikTok, and other video content – holds no secrets for them. They are very aware of the current job market and the scarcity of new talent, thus understanding their value. 'Hybrid' work is the norm for them, and they expect this mode of working to be standard. They also have to contend with many prejudices, which I'll address later in this chapter. They are the future, and in the 'love for talent' (our version of the 'war for talent', based on positive values and feelings), it is crucial to recognise and acknowledge them. Gen Z is also more conscious of life and society. They are true global citizens who fully recognise the importance of sustainability, even in the workplace. They are more pragmatic/entrepreneurial. They view technology as part of who they are. For them, the biggest challenge is 'real' connectivity: physical contact and face-to-face social interaction.

Gen Alpha (2010 – 2025): They are still at a distance from the job market, so I won't delve into them in this book.

As you can see, each generation grew up in a particular era and entered a specific type of job market. Consequently, each generation has its own talents and shortcomings. Therefore, we can only applaud a good mix in the workplace, which not only ensures diversity but also offers a broad range of knowledge, skills, and competencies necessary for a company's success and sustainability.

HOW TO KEEP GEN Z ON BOARD

To grasp the world of Gen Z, to understand what drives them and where their priorities lie, I spoke with Hugo Mutsaerts (lecturer-researcher in FM) from Breda University of Applied Sciences (BUas) and the Academy of Hotel and FM. He strongly focuses on education and guiding students, but he also specialises in advising and researching companies on organisational issues. A suitable interlocutor to gauge the themes that resonate with Gen Z, right?

Dealing with new generations in the business world is a phenomenon of all times. But today, this is coupled with scarcity in the job market. Gen Z, like every generation before them, is searching. But they are, more than previous generations, consciously seeking a job that aligns with their values. Hugo describes this with a commonly heard stereotype: "They are the Netflix generation: if it's not fun (anymore), they effortlessly switch to the next series." This aligns with their vision of work: they no longer position work as centrally as previous generations, which means they prioritise work differently as well.

Therefore, employers are trying to be more flexible and considering career guidance and well-being in the workplace. They want to attract and retain talent, but not by shielding them from every possible setback or disappointment because they also need to learn to deal with those, and leaving is usually not the best solution. But as an employer, you also need to accept that people leave and, therefore, you also need to ensure a healthy inflow of new talent. "But alongside inflow, you also need to strongly focus on progression," warns Hugo.

Hugo Mutsaerts

In other words, you need to ensure good career planning and training opportunities within the company. However, bear in mind the following: while a member of Gen X/Y stays in the same role for an average of five years, this has become an average of three years for Gen Z. If you want to retain a Gen Z employee for a longer period, it's best to provide sufficient challenges. On the other hand, you shouldn't be too obsessive about this. According to Hugo: "I am rather skeptical about the pursuit of 'retention'. In my opinion, it's mainly about good inflow, progression, and outflow of employees, rather than just desperately wanting to retain them. What's wrong with a colleague staying for three years if you could anticipate it in time? In my opinion, nothing."

From BUas's perspective, the internships offered are an 'eye opener'; they take Gen Z out of their bubble. You can talk endlessly about the field of work at university, but it's in practice, in the workplace, that you truly learn what this means. Hugo points out that you need to realise that Gen Z brings something new to companies. As long as you approach it appreciatively, they can create added value. "Because you must not underestimate this generation," emphasises Hugo, **"Gen Z is a strong generation with a lot of resilience."**

GEN Z SPEAKING

And how does Gen Z actually view the workplace? The best way to find out is simple: let's just ask them directly. Specifically, I've spoken with a few (former) students from BUas, Sophie Vos (graduating in 2024) and Annemarie Cortie (Project Manager at Facilicom Solutions, part of the Facilicom Group).

The first misconception they are eager to debunk is that, as 'digital natives', they don't want to come to the office. Naturally, they are the first generation to have grown up in a completely technology-driven society. But this has only led to a reconsideration of workplace culture. They go to the workplace precisely to meet people and collaborate. "Mind you, it's not about coming to the office to sit behind our screens for eight hours straight," Sophie points out immediately. They take responsibility for planning their own workday and see flexibility as paramount.

Sophie Vos

For Gen Z, work and personal life blend into a harmonious 'Work-Life Blend', where it's possible to exercise in the afternoon and pick up the kids after school, and then seamlessly continue working for a few more hours in the evening. The physical workplace thus takes on a new meaning: it should provide a pleasant atmosphere, inspire employees, and promote collaboration. Mobility also needs to be reconsidered in this new reality. This doesn't necessarily mean having a fancy company car, but it could also involve a train pass or other forms of public transportation. "These are more sustainable means of transportation that can help avoid traffic jams when visiting clients or projects," says Annemarie.

They also want to dispel the image of Gen Z as job hoppers who don't stay with the same employer for long. They are primarily looking for a company that shares the same values as they do. Additionally, the prospect of career opportunities after a period of three years is essential. High employee turnover in a company often reveals a lot about its operations, indicating a lack of alignment. They want the opportunity to continue developing themselves continuously; that's important. If this isn't offered, there are plenty of opportunities to seek those chances elsewhere. They also see new roles emerging in

Annemarie Cortie

the FM field, such as 'Chief Happiness Officer' (CHO), which is an interesting trend and offers them opportunities for the future. FM is well positioned to assist the CHO in satisfying and keeping employees happy by providing a workplace tailored to their specific needs.

Gen Z definitely sees the need for connection in the workplace with other generations, not only to learn from others but also because they believe older colleagues can also learn a lot from them. They recognise the danger that the 'always on' mentality poses to work-life balance, but they also see solutions. "Having a clear separation between the work phone and the personal phone is a good step," suggests Annemarie. This way, you can better disconnect from work and take better care of your mental well-being.

Gen Z is an environmentally-conscious generation, and they embody this in their norms and values, expecting the same from their employers. From an FM perspective, you can respond to this. However, this can only happen if the company's leadership is on board. They must emphasise the urgency of environmentally conscious and sustainable business practices and motivate and involve employees. Everyone should feel that it's more than just a marketing tool. This goes beyond the ESG narrative: an open attitude needs to be fostered across all themes and divisions between different generations. For example, you can ensure that members of Gen Z work side by side with other generations in cross-departmental project teams. Diversity benefits everyone, but at the same time, you should be able to identify with the company and the workplace. This isn't achieved solely through these project teams but also by, for instance, eliminating strict hierarchical lines and embracing an open feedback culture.

Finally, they both acknowledge that we live in a globalised society with a 24/7 economy that contradicts a '9 to 5' mentality. It's up to FM to optimise these flexible schedules as much as possible.

GEN Z AT WORK

Mathias De Roeck

I also found it interesting to assess Gen Z among some 'rookies' who have just started their facility careers. For example, last year I met Mathias De Roeck (Fleet & Facility Officer at Unit-T) and Rani Van Slembrouck (First Impression Manager & Facility Officer at Vyncke) at World Workplace Europe in Rotterdam. They both quickly realised that there remains a gap between theoretical approaches and the professional field. "The reality is much more complex than the theory taught in training," noted Rani. "Problem-solving and communication with different profiles and levels, including conflict resolution, are skills you quickly pick up in practice." Mathias added that the financial aspect shouldn't be underestimated: "Creating budgets is one thing, but translating and communicating them to management is a whole different skill."

Rani Van Slembrouck

They both observe that FM is a 'people business', so they spend a lot of time in the office. They want people to know them and understand what FM has to offer. They see this not only in themselves but also in their peers within the company. The social aspect definitely plays a role here. But especially for FM, physical presence is crucial for visibility and to keep a constant pulse on what's happening in the workplace. By collaborating with different generations, you understand their respective needs and can respond with solutions. "Also, look back and acknowledge what colleagues have done in the past," advises Mathias. "When changes are made in a project, make it discussable and explain why it could add value for them."

The hospitality of a company plays a significant role in whether they want to work there or not. This human aspect also matters greatly to them. "Colleagues and the work atmosphere contribute to your job satisfaction," says Rani. Mathias adds: "The challenge in the job is another factor. With all the projects on the agenda, every day is something different, and this keeps it interesting in my learning curve on the job."

Leadership plays a crucial role in translating societal challenges into the company and the workplace environment. "Think about hybrid working and the use of technology. Make this discussable and come up with a strategy and action plan. An open communication culture where employees are consulted is the way to go; it fosters engagement," says Mathias.

BECTON DICKINSON (BD)

Jari Van Neyghem

How do companies practically deal with this new generation? To find out, I consulted BD, an American multinational in medical technology with over 75,000 employees. Nathalie Cloet, Senior Facility Manager at BD and chair of the IFMA Belgium Chapter, told me that they have a separate working group in the Benelux region called 'Build'. To learn more about this, I sat down with Jari Van Neyghem, Supply Chain Financial Specialist and Koen Van Weyenbergh, Global Transportation Manager.

Their story perfectly illustrates how crucial leadership involvement is. In 2022, their General Manager in particular raised the question of how to engage

and retain Gen Z. HR Manager Renée Lefevre started working on this as part of BD's talent program 'Charge', which Koen was also involved in. After numerous workshops across different locations, they reached several conclusions. One of these was to establish a 'Next Gen' community called 'Build'. This, in turn, led to the creation of the project 'Build', with the involvement of some Gen Z individuals. Jari is part of this project team, and Koen is the coach. The goal is to give Gen Z a voice and involve them in decision-making.

Build stands for:
- Building the future
- Uniting the next generation within BD
- Improving BD as a company and workplace
- Linking our mission to the BD 2025 strategy
- Developing ourselves and others

This vision was concretely realised with a practical plan for 2024. This plan aims to increase the visibility of the Gen Z community in the Benelux, focusing on their value to the workplace and atmosphere. BD also emphasises Equity, Diversity, and Inclusion (EDI), of which 'Build' is a prime example. Four major initiatives have been outlined, with one being implemented each quarter.

- Panel discussion between different generations: how do they view each other and the workplace?
- Creating recreational spaces in the distribution centres in Olen and Temse, adapting the layout to include more meeting areas
- AI session across various sites: what is AI and how will it be used at BD?
- Financial podcast, providing financial insights about BD for 'dummies'.

BD understands the importance of two-way communication, and the community utilises the voice of all associates to take appropriate actions for an even better work environment. In this process, BD Benelux management is involved, ensuring adequate time allocation. The management of the Gen Z team members is also involved, ensuring they have the necessary time to dedicate. "The carrying capacity needs to be ensured," says Jari. As new colleagues join, they also have the opportunity to provide feedback to further enhance BD's workplace.

WHAT IS NEEDED FOR A SUSTAINABLE FUTURE PROOF WORK ENVIRONMENT?

Throughout my career, I have helped many companies with their future-proof work environment. Sometimes the emphasis was on FM, other times on technology. All these different projects made one thing very clear: every company is unique. Each company has its own vision and corporate culture. The biggest challenge often lies in examining and analysing whether their vision and culture are still future-proof. This concerns not only the physical work environment but also everything around it. With the following questions and answers, you as a facility professional can work towards creating that sustainable future-proof work environment.

HOW DO WE INVOLVE LEADERSHIP?

There needs to be a shift in the way we perceive leadership. 'Manage by results' is the management principle we must firmly focus on. This applies not only to Gen Z but to all generations working at your company. Ensure that you empower your employees to schedule their work independently. From FM, ensure that the physical workplace is accessible during the company's designated working hours (e.g., 7:00 am – 8:00 pm). This also impacts your service delivery, such as reception or security and the activation of alarms.

Another approach is to ensure that as FM, you also contribute to strategic company issues such as 'love for talent'. Your office contributes to the company's branding: when new talent arrives, they should immediately feel what your company stands for. Here, the design of the workplace adds value, as extensively discussed in chapter 3. Gen Z prefers a 'coaching' style of communication with a culture of direct and open feedback. As FM, you respond to this by ensuring a low-threshold culture with your workplace concept: the era of closed offices for executives is definitely over. Ensure you have formal and informal meeting places where you can have one-to-ones in a confidential setting. An open culture doesn't mean that everyone should hear everything or even be allowed to hear everything.

HOW DO WE ENSURE LIFELONG LEARNING?

Society is evolving at a rapid pace, causing our roles and tasks to continually change. This needs to be structurally supported by the company. The diversity of different generations in the workplace means that there is a lot of knowledge and skills available. You can maximise this by focusing on project work, creative sessions, informal meeting places, and more. As FM, you can help ensure that the available spaces stimulate collaboration, connection, and mutual learning. You should start by surveying the needs and requirements of your colleagues.

What's also important for a lifelong learning strategy is to focus on a personal development plan for everyone. This is primarily an HR matter, but for your own FM team, you should still remain closely involved. What are the functions today, how do you see the function evolving? What training do they need? All these questions need to be addressed. For example, think about data management? How can you provide insights to your FM managers or coordinators so they can develop a strategy? There are many pilot projects aiming to use AI in the form of chatbots for all employee-related queries. To manage this, you obviously need some basic knowledge. But the rapid technological evolution makes the human, the empathetic impact even more important. This will be a decisive factor in service delivery, so ensure your people are skilled in this and have enough empathy to focus on hospitality. Document this in your partnership with your FM service providers; ask them how they focus on training their people. You want your internal and external FM teams to be ready and capable of providing quality service in the workplace now and in the future.

WELL-BEING TAKES CENTRE STAGE

Burnout is still on the rise. It's important for your company to take this into account. For Gen Z, well-being is central to their lives. It's no longer just about the 'work-life balance'; Gen Zers oversee their entire lives and consider how work fits into it. This is what we call the 'work-life blend'. The previously mentioned 'always-on' mentality also deserves attention. Therefore, in FM, you can collaborate with HR & IT colleagues to establish a clear communication policy regarding expectations: when should someone be available and when not? In chapter 6, you'll find more about how to handle (digital) disconnection.

As FM, you can also help promote well-being in the workplace, for example, by making adjustments to the service offerings. A good example is TU Delft from chapter 7, where they have focused on vegetarian and vegan meals. Exercise and sports are also part of our well-being; it's not just about mental well-being. And again, FM can play an important role here, for example, with a 'start to run' programme or a padel session during lunch breaks.

WHAT HAVE WE LEARNED FROM THE WORKPLACE CONCEPT?

We discussed the workplace concept extensively in chapter 3. These insights help you design the ideal physical workspace. For Gen Z, it's about collaboration, meeting colleagues, and a workspace that contributes to the work atmosphere. It should be an inspiring place where the company's values are highlighted. And these values must be linked to Gen Z values; there must be a match. Focus on the individual, work across generations, don't create a one-size-fits-all office concept. Ensure that different tasks can be performed in the office and create a community.

HOW DOES ESG FIT INTO THIS STORY?

You read it right: the question is not WHETHER ESG fits into this story because that's not up for debate, but HOW it does. Gen Z has grown up with Greta Thunbergs climate strikes, and activists holding previous generations responsible for the state of our planet. From an FM perspective, you need to contribute to your organisation's sustainability policy. In chapter 7, we discussed a lot of practical examples. Make sure to communicate about this, not only internally but also externally via social media. These are positive stories that can have an impact on attracting future talent.

The DEI (Diversity, Equity & Inclusion) story is also not up for debate. It's not just about providing gender-neutral toilets but about involving all individuals in the workplace with all necessary attention to ethnic, cultural, and religious differences, as well as disabilities. Remember to provide prayer rooms, rest areas for young mothers, sensory-friendly spaces for hypersensitive individuals, and height-adjustable desks. FM can add a lot of value in this domain.

WHAT TECHNOLOGY DO THEY NEED?

Smartphones and soon Mixed Reality glasses (e.g. Apple Vision Pro) are indispensable in our work environment, how we communicate, and how we plan and carry out our work. In chapter 4, we discussed the 'employee journey' (from an FM perspective) and the 'employee experience', and how technology can support this. For FM, technology serves, among other things, to make your facility services available to your colleagues in a simple way. Think of a simple app where you can create tickets, order lunch, see where your colleagues are working today, or reserve a charging point for your car. In the physical workplace, technology is also indispensable, for example, to organise hybrid meetings where both video and audio quality are top-notch.

There are few surprising answers in this last section; I realise that all too well. Not least because we see many of the insights discussed earlier recurring here. But this overview makes it manageable and easy for you to get started within your company, so you can build a workplace that appeals to Gen Z and meets their expectations for the workplace of tomorrow and the future.

"FOR GEN Z, WELL-BEING IS CENTRAL TO THEIR LIVES. IT'S NO LONGER JUST ABOUT THE 'WORK-LIFE BALANCE': GEN ZERS OVERSEE THEIR ENTIRE LIVES AND CONSIDER HOW WORK FITS INTO IT. THIS IS WHAT WE CALL THE 'WORK-LIFE BLEND.'"

7 STEPS TO SUCCESS

1. Who are the generations in your workforce? Take a snapshot.
2. Involve your leadership, start a project group on generational diversity in the workplace.
3. Have discussions with HR about lifelong learning.
4. Incorporate well-being into your service offering.
5. Focus on sustainability (ESG / DEI) as part of your company branding.
6. Provide the right tools for the ideal employee journey.
7. Evaluate your current workplace concept and compare it with future needs.

CHAPTER 10

A GLIMPSE INTO THE FUTURE

Since my youth, I've had a special interest in what the future would bring. Science fiction movies and TV series like 'Star Trek' sparked my imagination excessively. How cool would it be if we could simply say "Beam me up, Scotty!" to be instantly teleported to your destination? Today, I find this idea more appealing than ever, with the increasing traffic jams and mobility issues year after year. But teleportation won't be for our generation. Nonetheless, I continue to follow what is happening around us with great interest, to assess what can be applied in FM in the short, medium and long term.

Typically, you see innovative developments first emerging in your own private environment and only later being implemented in a business context. Think about how streaming platforms use AI: they analyse the viewing behaviour of all their users, not only to make suggestions – "People who watched this series also like to watch etc." – but also to study which new content they should make in which region, based on the specific viewing behaviour in those regions. Such things are perfectly applicable in an FM context: "People who book this meeting room also like to reserve a pointer for their presentations. Would you like to reserve that too?"

But rest assured: I don't want to overwhelm you with cool technical innovations that may or may not enter our workplace in the distant future. We will mainly discuss developments that have already surfaced here and there and are almost ready for the big breakthrough – in our FM market and our workplace too. And at the same time, you'll get the necessary tips to prepare for this future. We'll look at this future from two perspectives: on the one hand, the 'hard' angle of technology, and on the other hand, the 'soft' approach that focuses more on humans. From both angles, a lot of changes are underway.

So, in this chapter, we'll talk about our VUCA world and how FM can use innovation to deal with it. We'll get acquainted with the Metaverse, AI, and Super Apps. And from the 'soft' angle, we'll learn why we should expect an even greater talent shortage, but also how the Chief Happiness Officer impacts the well-being of our employees.

THE 'VUCA' WORLD OF FM

The preceding chapters have partly clarified it: we live in a 'VUCA' world. And it seems that it will become even more VUCA in the future. For those less familiar with the jargon, VUCA stands for Volatility, Uncertainty, Complexity, and Ambiguity. It's an acronym used to describe the rapidly changing and unpredictable nature of today's business and socital environment.

- **Volatility:** Refers to the speed and magnitude of changes. In a VUCA world, events and circumstances can shift quickly and unexpectedly.
- **Uncertainty:** Indicates the limited predictability of events. In an uncertain environment, it's difficult to accurately predict future developments.
- **Complexity:** Refers to the many interconnected factors and uncertainties that complicate decision-making. Problems and situations are often characterised by multiple interrelated variables and unclear causal relationships.
- **Ambiguity:** Means that information can have multiple interpretations, making decision-making difficult. In a VUCA environment, it's not always clear what's going on or what the best actions are.

Organisations and individuals aware of the VUCA reality strive to be flexible, adaptive, and resilient to effectively deal with the constant changes and uncertainty in their environment.

Jos Duchamps

How can we now deal with this complex matter from an FM perspective? And what impact does this have on our workplace environment? I consulted one of the founders of IFMA Belgium and the current chairman of IFMA EMEA, Jos Duchamps (also Managing Partner of PROCOS Group). First and foremost, innovation in FM must be viewed at different levels: operational, tactical, and strategic. Jos suggests "To create support, you always need to introduce innovation through the strategic level. There must be added value for the organisation from a broad business perspective."

The next step is to bring together the right parties, Jos continues. "Look at the concept of hybrid working; for this you need HR to develop a good policy. 'Changing the way we work' is also innovative and FM plays a key role here." Another aspect that will be heavily invested in over the coming years is the energy transition and how you can take charge of energy yourself, relying less on the uncertain external world: "Think about installing wind turbines, solar panels (if they're not already there), create your own energy park if you get the chance." On a tactical level, for example, BIM for FM adds value when it comes to new buildings or renovations. This can contribute to 'the building passport' where all information about the building is stored. By clearly and uniformly centralising all this information and thus eliminating possible ambiguity, you're already partially getting rid of the 'U' from VUCA, the uncertainty. The next step could then be to look at how you can make your building 'smarter'.

The final level is the operational level, where we are dealing with challenges such as a shortage of trained and qualified personnel. Utilising cobots and robots can offer a solution here, for example, in cleaning tasks. So, it's not just about implementing technology; it's more about examining the thinking processes and the entire FM management within the organisation.

"I also want to make it clear that there is a difference between innovation on the one hand and integrating new technology into our FM industry on the other hand," says Jos. "With new technology, you always need to be able to demonstrate its added value. They are often not 'big bang' implementations but rather a series of smaller projects that make a real contribution. Innovation, on the other hand, should be a 'never-ending story'. This needs to be embedded in the company's culture. Innovation is done step-by-step but continuously. From an FM perspective, you should also look at developments in other sectors such as banking, industry, and logistics, and investigate whether these can add value to our own FM environment. Innovation is not just something for FM; it's a company-wide issue. Make sure you can participate in these multidisciplinary discussions."

Jos believes it is everyone's responsibility to focus on innovation. "On the one hand, it comes from the demand side: companies outsourcing services should specify that they expect certain innovative measures in the service provision. On the other hand, it's the FM service providers who must continue to develop their service offerings. They need to offer innovation to their clients. This can stimulate enough change in the FM market. And of course, professional federations like IFMA – with trend reports, site visits, etc. – play an important role in further supporting the FM community."

Innovation is therefore an important weapon against VUCA. But that doesn't mean you should now go 100% into innovation in all areas. A big bang approach often leads to even more uncertainty among employees. So try not to rush, look at the long term, and avoid a purely top-down approach. Work with pilot projects and involve multidisciplinary teams. This will contribute to greater acceptance and therefore the success of innovation in your company. And don't forget: shake off that 'Calimero' image and make sure your backpack is full to discuss innovation at a strategic level!

THE OFFICE IS DEAD! WELCOME THE METAVERSE

Figure 10.1 : Example photo of the Metaverse

By now, it will not surprise anyone that I spent a lot of time in my youth (I certainly wouldn't call it wasted) gaming. Back then, these were still very classic 2D games that you could play alone or at best with two people on a console. We had never heard of online games, let alone the Metaverse. And our parents just went to the office every day. How different our world looks today. Online gaming has become the standard, and AR (Augmented Reality) and VR (Virtual Reality) are increasingly peeking around the corner. The Metaverse will probably first penetrate the gaming world and find its way into other private applications. But sooner or later, we will also enter virtual offices and hold 'meta' meetings in a business context. And that can happen quickly. A few years ago, no one thought we would all be working from home and talking to our screens, did they? So why not do this in a pleasant 3D environment where you add an extra dimension, namely an immersive experience?

The term 'Metaverse' refers to an extensive virtual universe consisting of multiple interconnected digital worlds. In the Metaverse, people can communicate via digital avatars, engage in social interactions, participate in activities, and even conduct economic transactions. The concept goes beyond traditional virtual worlds and online platforms, and the idea is that the Metaverse provides a seamless and cohesive experience in which users can freely move between different virtual environments.

Pieter Van Leugenhagen

I spoke with my good friend Pieter Van Leugenhagen, who is an authority on the Metaverse. He is the Co-founder and Managing Partner of the company Yondr, which focused on the Metaverse during the pandemic and what this could mean for the business world. For example, they built an environment for Ikea and the European Commission, where colleagues could meet each other in virtual meeting rooms as avatars. You create the feeling that you can interact with the entire group. It is a many-to-many form of communication, which also makes it ideal for organising virtual events.

Pieter Van Leugenhagen is convinced that the Metaverse will be an integral part of the future workplace: "Hybrid working will continue, and everyone is looking for the best way to collaborate. To work interactively and connectively as an alternative to physical meetings, the 3D world of the Metaverse can be very interesting. It's about that convergence of the physical and virtual world within the three-dimensional context of collaboration. This can be an avatar attending a call in the real world from their virtual world, but it can also be a physical person entering the virtual world via a video window."

The new generations entering the job market consider this a normal platform for interaction, from their gaming background or the performances they've seen of their favourite artists in the Metaverse. For many people (older generations), it takes some adjustment to work with avatars (fictional digital characters) and a cartoonish interface. The technology already exists to digitise your physical person, but this technology isn't mature enough yet to go mainstream. Looking at developments like Microsoft's Mesh for Teams, you can now have your company's meeting rooms in the Metaverse and collaborate with your avatar in this new Teams environment. Even in the development of new buildings, there's a focus on 'digital twins' in the Metaverse. Companies like BMW and Siemens are heavily involved, digitally constructing the factories of the future to first test interventions for sustainability and productivity virtually before going 'live'. These models can also be used for training and later for maintenance on installations.

While everyone today is mainly focused on AI, the development of Metaverse technology continues steadily, notes Pieter: "Just look at the many announcements around MR (Mixed Reality) headsets by tech leaders like Meta, Samsung, and Lenovo. Apple even calls them Spatial Computers. If these glasses become mainstream, they'll become a standard item in the workplace of the future." He also gives this advice: "Consider Metaverse technology as something that can add value to your company. Think about the ecological footprint and business travel, inviting external visitors to your virtual creative lab, inviting customers to a virtual event. Of course, it must fit the culture and vision of your company. It should be part of your innovation process so you can experiment with it and put it into practice."

AI MAKES JOBS REDUNDANT, BUT NOT PEOPLE

Will AI take over our jobs to address the 'war for talent' or will it stimulate unemployment? Perhaps this needs to be a bit more nuanced. With ChatGPT, we're paving a new path towards providing tools at a more accessible level. How can this be integrated into the FM field? Mieke De Ketelaere, keynote speaker at IFMA Belgium's (re)launch event, wrote an extremely interesting book on this topic 'Wanted: Human-AI translators'. It clearly states that AI is on the rise and will be indispensable in many applications in the future. But the current level of AI is best described as that of a toddler in a human life. So we still have a long way to go.

What is AI exactly? These are computer systems that learn, make decisions, and execute them independently. One application of this is ChatGPT. This is a chatbot with artificial intelligence developed in the USA by the company OpenAI.

In the short term, I see AI further integrated into the following FM domains: automating facility processes, improving employee experience, FM service desk optimisation, and FM service providers, knowledge database.

Automating facility processes.

Data is king! Believers in digital twins, smart buildings, and IoT will rejoice. With the help of AI and smart algorithms, entire facility processes can be automated from A to Z. This saves a lot in planning and follow-up. For example, if the temperature in a meeting room exceeds 23°C, this can trigger an alarm and create a work order immediately; since this is for a building in Antwerp, the IWMS (Integrated Workplace Management System) knows which service provider should be assigned. The technician then receives the work order on his smartphone and can proceed with it. Of course, you can go much further by linking BMS (Building Management Systems) with IWMS. However, this requires the AI system to be linked to make 'smart' decisions based on data and initiate the right processes.

Improving the employee experience

Everyone is struggling to get their employees back to the workplace. We can do this by enhancing the 'employee experience'. This has been used in B2C applications for much longer. Just think of booking.com when planning a trip. It will make recommendations based on your preferences and previously booked trips. If we were to extend this AI application to the workplace so that you could receive recommendations in advance, wouldn't this make everything much easier? You open the app and immediately receive some suggestions. "Hey Tom, how are you? Are you coming to the office? Well, then we can recommend the workspace on the third floor of the west wing. I see that you want to reserve the whole day. Can I go ahead and reserve the chicken poké bowl in the company restaurant for you?"

Some people will like this, others won't. If it's based on your own previous experiences and collected data, I can imagine this would improve the employee experience. With GDPR rules in place, it might take a while before this becomes operational.

Optimising the FM service desk

The FM service desk is the focal point of the facility organisation, the beating heart. As mentioned earlier, processes can be automated, and AI can be applied to the entire CWIS (complaints, wishes, information, service disruption) system. This, once again, results in an efficiency gain in the scheduling of service tickets. And why not introduce a smart chatbot that colleagues can rely on? Through data, it becomes smarter over time and can provide increasingly better answers regarding the specificity of buildings and the scope of related facility services. This, in turn, leads to the domain discussed above: enhancing employee experience.

FM service providers, knowledge base

There has been a long-standing shortage in the job market of good technical profiles as well as of operational staff for soft services. Not everyone has the same knowledge and experience, so how can we support people and impart knowledge through technology? When you need to carry out an intervention, your first point of contact is your AI service desk. Here, you could again work with a knowledge base to which AI is applied. It becomes smarter with the questions asked, including those posed by technicians. By providing 'augmented reality' glasses and linking them to the digital twin (BIM) narrative, we can even use AR (augmented reality) to ensure that individuals on the work floor can immediately see the information and know what action they need to take. Of course, everything starts with training, certificates and competencies, but these additional capabilities can assist in deploying multidisciplinary teams.

We still have a long way to go. The question of whether the necessary AI technology exists is no longer the right question. The question is: How do we use it and deploy it optimally?

CYBERSECURITY

With all new technology, new threats emerge as well. Therefore, cybersecurity, the protection of our digital environment, will play a crucial role, now and even more so in the future.

I had an engaging conversation with Jeffrey Saunders, CEO of Nordic Foresight and also CTO of Denmark's National Defence Technology Centre, about current and future cyber threats. In short, he's the ideal person to question on the topic.

In a world that is fully interconnected, where data is generated everywhere, cybersecurity deserves a prominent role as it makes our work environment and FM safer. "The most common things we immediately think of are all IT devices (smartphone, tablet, laptop, etc.) that can pose a potential threat," says Jeffrey, "But this is more for our IT friends. In the real estate and FM world, we have been slower to anticipate digitalisation and all that comes with it. It should not surprise us then that we have only started to look at the concept of cybersecurity and to attach the necessary importance to it more recently. If we consider that our work environment and buildings are designed for 20 to 30 years, then you also need to carefully consider which systems you are going to integrate into them and how they can be kept up to date. In older buildings, you often have outdated systems; let's say a BMS (building management system), which works stand-alone and with little or no security. If these systems get an upgrade and are connected in a platform mindset, then this link can be a potential risk."

Jeffrey Saunders

Hackers always seek the easiest way to gain access to something. If they can control the BMS system remotely, this can create a very tricky situation. This can happen through the HVAC system, but also through other entry points, warns Jeffrey: "Think about security systems and access control. You don't want to leave an 'open door' at your company. And imagine if you work in the financial sector, then this becomes even more alarming. But even the operation of elevators can be disrupted, causing people to get stuck. And so we could go on and on. That's the big difference; IT infrastructure and software need renewal every two to three years or to regularly receive updates to keep up with potential risks. With outdated systems in buildings, it's different, and we need to be aware of that."

These may seem like scenarios from cheap science fiction stories and therefore far from us. But actually, this can already happen now, and the threat will increase month by month. What can we do now to reduce that threat? Start as an FM professional by mapping out which systems you have, where data is located, and what the risk would be if this system were to fail or if these data were lost. We have already discussed this in chapter 4 for the digital environment in general, and it's no different for cybersecurity. Take your snapshot and determine where you as an FM professional can add value.

However, security doesn't stop with the digital world; it's just as important in the physical world, though nowadays they are increasingly intertwined. If someone is fired in your organisation, they should not have physical access to the building any-more, but they should also no longer have access to the data or systems. This is a task that you as an FM professional need to take up with HR, security, and IT. Cyber-security requires an integrated approach; you don't need to become an IT expert as an FM professional, but you do need to sit around the table with the stakeholders. And, of course, the sector you work in also plays a role in your approach to (cy-ber)security; the financial sector is an example where security standards are sig-nificantly higher. Also, consider the frequency of meetings with your IT security team to discuss global security aspects. Weekly, monthly, quarterly, or not yet? Beyond internal collaboration, partnering with external FM stakeholders is cru-cial. Ensure you check with them how they perceive cybersecurity and how they can ensure its optimal maintenance within your organisation. Make sure they can provide certificates such as ISO 27001 or ISA 62443 (the standard for Opera-tions Technologies). The aim of ISO 27001 is to provide a structured framework for protecting confidential information and ensuring the availability, integrity, and confidentiality of information within an organisation. It applies to all types of organisation, regardless of size or nature, and can be used to ensure information security across various sectors.

Keep in mind that both IT (Information Technology) and OT (Operational Tech-nology) systems may be present, each with different regulations and standards. It will be quite a task to further centralise and align all these systems. Don't forget about the landlord or real estate manager: What processes and systems do they control, and how can they ensure safety? In short, when creating your snapshot, approach it from different angles, both internally and externally. This provides a comprehensive view and enables further action.

We also need to ensure continuous training for our FM colleagues so they become aware of potential risks. All too often, breaches are caused by human error. En-sure people understand their responsibility and the actions they need to take in the event of a breach, regardless of their role, whether executive or coordinating. And yes, AI will play a bigger role in cybersecurity in the future. Hackers are us-ing AI to launch more efficient attacks, and their breaches will have a much more significant impact once they penetrate systems. Their algorithms can learn from their actions and adapt. It's somewhat alarming, but essential to prepare for. For-tunately, cybersecurity companies have also embraced AI, making the detection of new threats more efficient. Nevertheless, it remains an extremely important focal point.

"Awareness in the FM sector is increasing and will continue to do so in the coming years as cyberattacks become more prevalent. Therefore, make sure it's alive in your organisation," concludes Jeffrey.

SKILLS, SKILLS, SKILLS

As noticed earlier in this chapter, society is changing faster than ever before. And, naturally, our job market is changing along with it, at the same rapid pace. What impact does this have on the world of FM? The same as in other sectors: the shortage of resources worsens year by year, and we don't see any change coming in the near future. In our sector, we're also constantly searching for the 'white raven', the person who can do everything: from chores to managing the facility helpdesk, budgeting, interpreting data, and so on.

Because you rarely encounter such white ravens on the job market, there's really only one option: you create that multi-talent yourself. And lifelong learning will play an important role here. How else can you make a difference? In many ways, actually.

Automate routine tasks

Many tasks that recur regularly can now be 'automated', and fortunately so. This allows us to focus on tasks that are more challenging and contribute to our job satisfaction. With many processes automated at your FM Service Desk, you can efficiently assign service tickets to the right colleagues or partners. You can focus on the essence, on questions like: What is the quality of our service and how can I improve it? Automation is also possible in operational functions such as cleaning; cobots and robots have been part of the daily cleaning team in many companies for quite some time now. This allows cleaners to focus on more complex tasks, which only improves the service. This trend towards more focus on challenging and complex tasks clearly continues into the future. So make sure to guide your people, including through training, to take on these jobs.

Embrace IT

A Facility Manager is known as a generalist with a broad spectrum who surrounds themselves with specialists. During a presentation by Professor Jean-Pierre Segers (Brains & Trees) at an event by IFMA Belgium, the skills and competencies the Facility Manager will need in the future were examined. How do we shape our people into the 'multi-skilled' professionals that FM needs? IT will be an essential part of this. You don't need to become an IT expert, but you do need to delve into the subject and keep up with market developments. Data management, IoT, smart buildings, FM platforms etc.: you don't necessarily need to know the bits and bytes, but you need to understand the principles and realise what these technologies can bring as added value in your workplace environment. Make sure to connect with your FM colleagues in other organisations, look for use cases, and learn from each other.

Crossing generations

Today, we have four generations in the workplace: the Boomer, Gen X, Gen Y, and Gen Z. And soon, Gen Alpha will join them. There is so much knowledge within these cohorts, and companies need to capitalise on it. Ensure you create multidisciplinary teams where knowledge sharing is the norm. Don't confine this to the traditional model where older individuals mentor younger ones, as learning goes both ways. Gen Z are 'digital natives' capable of imparting valuable skills to other generations in the workplace. Ensure people don't remain in their silos by investing in knowledge sharing and enriching your workspace. This will ultimately lead to a more pleasant work atmosphere where people appreciate and understand each other better. Approaching facility issues from various perspectives increases the likelihood of inspiring solutions beneficial to all.

Emphasising empathy and experience

Perhaps the most crucial advice from this list: prioritise empathy and experience. Just as we increasingly rely on technology and IT, the human factor becomes more critical than ever. This holds true in FM as well. Ensure people are trained to show respect and attention to how the workspace environment is managed. Embed 'hospitality' into your company culture and integrate it into your facility services. Make people proud to be part of the facility team, knowing they contribute daily to the company's core processes. It starts with a simple question on the work floor: "How are you doing?" It may sound trivial, but it's incredibly important – everyone carries their own emotional baggage and personal experiences every day. FM is a 'people business'; prioritise empathy and experience!

Lifelong learning

Companies need to invest even more in lifelong learning, and this commitment must come from the management. Often, you hear: "It's too busy now; we'll consider training after projects are completed." But we all know it won't get any less busy. You have to create that space so people can further develop themselves. This fosters a stronger connection with the company and reduces the likelihood of employees seeking opportunities elsewhere. Create a plan for your employees in the short, medium, and long term; it simplifies planning and provides perspective for the employee. Training and guidance should be integral parts of career planning.

Ultimately, this cultivates individuals who continually improve themselves, creating the rare talent you're seeking. However, the well-being of employees should remain central. Transform the 'war for talent' into a 'love for talent' by continuously supporting employees' development, strengthening their bond with the company.

Each aspect above could be the subject of a separate book. The list of skills and competencies required in our beloved FM industry is impressive. According to IFMA's Global Job Task Analysis (GJTA), successful Facility Managers need skills in sustainability, operations & maintenance, project management, leadership & strategy, communications, performance & quality, finance & business, information & technology management, occupancy & human factors, real estate, and risk management. Any individual who possesses all these skills is, in my opinion, yet to be found. However, continuous effort is essential.

Consider what you need to prepare for the future, whether it's sustainability, technology, AI, conflict resolution, or other areas. Make your path and schedule your training to become a future-proof, multi-skilled FM professional!

Hannah Wilson: "Skills from other disciplines are also needed"

The above advice is not only my opinion, but also endorsed by international experts like Hannah Wilson, Senior Researcher in Business Administration at Liverpool John Moores University. Hannah has contributed to numerous studies on workplace and workplace psychology from the perspective of employees, and their impact on workplace design and management. "We gradually realised the importance of placing FM at the management level rather than under technology and administration," says Hannah. "FM needs to become part of the strategic setting. In recent years, there has been a (r)evolution; in the past, FM and the workplace were viewed from a building perspective, then technology was added, and in recent years, the focus has been on the human element, the employee. This allows you to contribute to the 'employee experience'."

As a result, FM is moving further away from the traditional approach of the construction sector, notes Hannah: "There is more focus on leadership and management where FM and the workplace can make a positive contribution. People working in FM or deciding to start in FM will perform different roles in their professional careers. By linking your career to your development plan, you will build a 'portfolio' of skills. Due to constantly changing challenges, you will need to keep learning continuously."

"Therefore, there is a constant need for upskilling," continues Hannah. "And this upskilling should not be limited to our own field but should also be sought in other disciplines such as HR. Think of cognitive & creative skills, communication & teamworking skills. If we want to bridge the gap between the FM market and FM education, there must be more collaboration at various levels. Students should not only understand the FM sector but also the adjacent sectors, such as HR, IT and real estate. And they must understand how businesses operate in general. And since FM should serve employees, they must also understand how employees view their 'employee journey' and the 'employee experience', knowing that FM and the workplace can contribute to this."

Experienced FM professionals can also contribute to education, and according to Hannah, this is everyone's responsibility: "Try to connect with universities, colleges, professional associations (IWFM, EuroFM). Make sure to share use cases with the FM community, show different perspectives, and contribute to change in the FM market."

"Education should also focus on change management so that students can bring different perspectives to the field when they enter the workforce," concludes Hannah.

More than ever, the human element takes centre stage in business operations; when employees are happy, they feel more connected to the company. We discussed this extensively in chapter 6, and this trend is undoubtedly set to continue in the coming years. Companies can respond to this in various ways, but one of the most intriguing solutions we foresee having a bright future is the appointment of a 'Chief Happiness Officer' (CHO).

A Chief Happiness Officer's primary mission is to contribute to promoting the well-being and satisfaction of employees within an organisation. When a CHO collaborates with FM, it can have a positive impact on the workplace and the overall working environment. Shouldn't the CHO's role simply be entrusted to an FM professional? Or could the FM professional thrive best in the role as a 'facilitator' who optimally supports the CHO's objectives? The conclusion remains the same in any case: FM and CHO are inherently linked. You'll notice this naturally when you review the focus areas of a CHO: many of these are already part of the FM or Workplace Experience Manager's responsibilities.

Creating a positive work environment

The CHO can collaborate with FM to create a work environment conducive to positive interactions and an overall good atmosphere. This can translate concretely into designing communal spaces, introducing natural light, implementing colour psychology, and creating relaxation zones.

Flexible work environment

A CHO can strive for more flexibility in the workplace, for example, by promoting telecommuting, flexible working hours, and creating co-working spaces. FM can contribute to this by considering an adapted framework that allows for both flexibility and connectivity. The necessary technologies and spaces ensure a good employee experience in a digital and hybrid work environment. According to a study by Robert Half (salary guide/flexibility), hybrid working has a positive impact on well-being (63%), motivation (59%), and productivity (50%).

Innovative office designs

Collaboration between the CHO and FM can lead to innovative office designs that promote openness, collaboration, and creativity. This may include the use of ergonomic furniture, green plants, and spaces for informal gatherings.

Listening to employees

A CHO can serve as a bridge between employees and FM, acting as 'the spider in the web', the 'whistleblower' who captures and passes on employees' needs and feedback about the workplace to the FM team. By organising regular surveys and feedback sessions, the CHO can gather information to improve facilities and the work environment. The CHO can also ensure a good approach to change management. By having the right vision, buy-in, resources, knowledge, action, and assurance, you can ensure that change results in success, as Mary Lippitt expresses in 'The Managing Complex Change Model'.

Whether someone is given the title Chief Happiness Officer or not ultimately matters less. What is important is that the themes falling under the jurisdiction of such a CHO are indeed incorporated within your company. As an FM professional, you can be a driving force in contributing to the happiness in your workplace environment!

'A CHO CAN SERVE AS A BRIDGE BETWEEN EMPLOYEES AND FM, ACTING AS 'THE SPIDER IN THE WEB', THE 'WHISTLEBLOWER' WHO CAPTURES AND PASSES ON EMPLOYEES' NEEDS AND FEEDBACK ABOUT THE WORKPLACE TO THE FM TEAM'

7 STEPS TO SUCCESS

1. Create support for innovation at the strategic, tactical, and operational levels.
2. Consult with your peers and FM service Providers to gather innovative use cases.
3. Avoid the 'big bang' approach, work with pilot projects, and involve a multi-disciplinary team.
4. Embrace new technologies such as Virtual Reality, Augmented Reality, Metaverse, and AI. Assess where these can add value in your organisation.
5. Put cybersecurity on the agenda and map out your facility's critical points.
6. Lifelong learning is for everyone; create your training plan to become a multi-skilled FM professional.
7. Collaborate with HR to see how FM can contribute to the happiness of your colleagues.

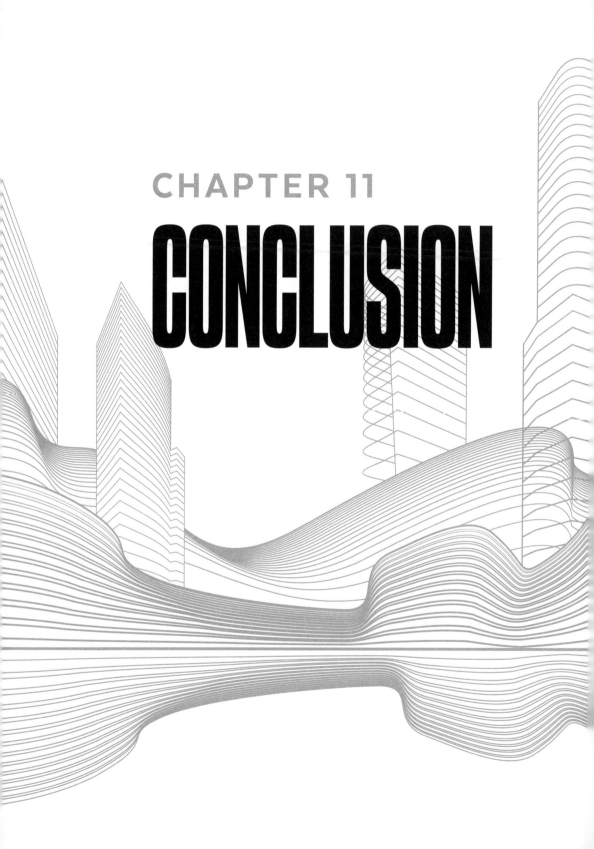

CHAPTER 11

CONCLUSION

I t's a wrap! Together we've covered all the facets of FM and workplace experience. All the important topics were addressed in the various chapters, each concluded with '7 steps to success' for those who want to take action in the new workplace. And how better to conclude this tour through many buildings and all other aspects of our workplace than with a helicopter ride? Yes, in this chapter, I would like to offer you all the topics once again from a 'helicopter view'– to review the many perspectives from the different chapters, to briefly reiterate how you can start 'to create your sustainable and future-proof work environment'. And because helicopter rides are just fun, right?

THE CHALLENGES

The biggest change we've experienced is the shift of focus from the building to the human. You need to consider both internal and external challenges and take the 4 Ps as guidance: People, Places, Performance & Planet. In the internal challenges, your company culture plays a role, and with Sinek's model (Why, How, What), you can determine the added value FM and your workplace environment have in your company. For external challenges in society, you can use the DESTEP methodology to gain more insight into the specific region you are in.

DATA MANAGEMENT

There has never been as much data generated as there is now, and FM can also work with it. Converting the right data into usable insights, which in turn lead to concrete action(s) – that's what it's all about. That's why it's best to start with this question: What do we as Facility Managers want to measure? Start by creating a clear data management strategy. Also, consider this from the role you are active in, as a Facility Manager, as an FM service provider, as a real estate manager/developer. Workplace occupancy seems like an ideal starting point to practically start shaping your real estate strategy for the future. Also, consider what technology you want to use to capture data: sensors, IoT etc.

HYBRID WORKING

As far as I'm concerned, the term 'hybrid' working can go out the window. It's simply the way we work today. In the new work reality, companies adopt a work philosophy and practice focused on providing more flexibility and autonomy to employees, partly by making better use of available technology. The objective is twofold: on the one hand, improving work performance, and on the other hand, increasing employee satisfaction. Consider how you currently approach 'activity-based working' and 'event-based working' and how you intend to further shape this in the future. When undertaking such strategic exercises and changes, there's one golden rule: always incorporate change management into developing a new office concept throughout the entire process.

TECHNOLOGY

You need to be aware of the available technology. Let's be clear, technology itself is not the goal; it's a support to solve issues and lead us to a better workplace. Reflect on where technology can support you: optimising your resources, enhancing building user comfort, centralising data and turning it into business intelligence, utilising real-time data for agile service delivery. Explore which technology or platform concept can support you: Integrated Workplace Management System (IWMS), smart buildings, BIM, Digital Twin etc. Most importantly, start by defining your 'use case' – why you want to do it and what you aim to achieve – and assess what you already have in place before venturing into the market.

COLLABORATION

Ensure that for each level – operational, tactical, and strategic – you register all the objectives that can help you achieve them, and outline how you plan to implement them in the short, medium, and long term. Once you've done this exercise, you'll be better equipped to convince others that you can and should play this role at every level. As an FM professional, you're the linchpin. You need to build bridges between FM, your colleagues, other departments, your end clients, and your FM service providers. Operate based on the 'know-like-trust' concept: make sure your stakeholders first get to know FM, then appreciate it, and eventually trust it. From then on, FM naturally ascends to a higher level.

WELL-BEING

To build that optimal workplace experience, you must also understand precisely what employees desire, what they need. This closely aligns with Human Resources (HR), with the team constantly working on the well-being and happiness of all the talent present. From the perspective of psychosocial risks, you can mainly impact working conditions. But even in optimising labour relations, the Facility Manager can play a role by providing a work environment that can facilitate and improve relationships between colleagues, with customers, and with management. If you aim to keep employees satisfied and happy in their workplace, you must consider the various facets of an employee. We use the so-called 3 Bs for this: brain, belonging, and balance. When you address all three dimensions, you'll notice that your employees are more motivated, and you can even start talking about employee happiness.

ESG IN THE WORKPLACE

In every company, in every sector, you can no longer ignore it: you must and will engage in environmentally conscious and sustainable business practices. Every company, small or large, will now or in the very near future need to have a sustainability strategy. When selecting suppliers or forming partnerships, there will increasingly be inquiries about this strategy before any collaboration takes place. To make reporting on sustainability within the EU as accurate and consistent as possible, the European Commission has released the European Sustainability Reporting Standards (ESRS). As an FM, consider the following categories to get started: certification for your building, energy consumption, renewable energy sources, fleet management, waste management, landscaping, and much more. Focus on sustainable business practices and don't forget the 'social' aspect.

AGILE SERVICE DELIVERY

To achieve 'agile service delivery', you must first measure the maturity of your facility organisation and assess which phase you are in with your contract models. Are you in the 'resource-oriented contract', 'result-oriented contract', or 'data-driven contract' phase? This will determine your flexibility and whether you can speak of Facility as a Service (FaaS). Providing data to your FM service provider is essential here to transition to data-driven contracts. How you wish to outsource depends on which model aligns best with your company and your facility organisation, ranging from 'single services' to 'integrated FM'. Of course, everything also depends on how much coordination and management you have in-house and what you can handle regarding contract management. Practice 'expectation management' with your end customers, your management, and your colleagues from other departments. This will provide the specifications you need for your facility services. It is an art to balance quality, added value, and budget.

GENERATIONS IN THE WORKPLACE

Currently, there are four generations active in the workplace: Boomers, Gen X, Gen Y, and Gen Z. This chapter does not limit itself to Gen Z but addresses all generations working in your company. There needs to be a shift in the way leadership is viewed. 'Manage by results' is the card to be played. Ensure that you give your employees the autonomy to schedule their work themselves and the flexibility to do so within working hours. But there are other focal points to create your sustainable, future-proof workplace. Focus on lifelong learning, prioritise well-being in your organisation, adapt your workplace concept, focus on sustainability and inclusion. Explore how technology can support these focal points.

A GLIMPSE INTO THE FUTURE

To focus on innovation, it is necessary to create support at both the strategic, tactical, and operational levels. Look for innovative use cases among your 'peers' and partners; they should enable you to apply these things in your facility organisation and workplace. Start with a pilot project and involve a multidisciplinary team. The 'big bang' approach does not work, so keep that in mind. Ensure you have a keen interest in new technology coming our way, such as Virtual Reality, Augmented Reality, Metaverse and AI etc. Always consider where and how this could add value within your organisation. With new technology and connectivity come new risks, so cybersecurity should also be on your agenda. Identify the critical points and make a plan. As for 'soft skills', lifelong learning is a basic requirement for everyone. We need to focus on our future to become a multi-skilled FM professional!

I hope you enjoyed reading the book as much as I enjoyed writing it. You'll find plenty of building blocks to create your sustainable and future-proof work environment. Therefore, I'd like to conclude with one of my favourite quotes from Richard Branson: "Screw it, let's do it!"

ACKNOWLEDGEMENTS

FAMILY & FRIENDS ABOVE ALL!

My deepest gratitude goes out to my family. To my wife, Kathleen, who has had to exercise a lot of patience all those times I was lost in thought or quickly scribbling a blueprint in my notebook during the many preparatory sessions and meetings with FM professionals. She ensured I could write this book, and that is invaluable. A thousand thanks for your support and love! Of course, also to my children who have been very patient and respectful during the busy writing process. Thank you Birthe and Bent!

To my family and in-laws, especially my mother Ingrid and her partner Wilfried, my sister Evy, and my brother-in-law Robert (aka Pros), for their interest and encouraging words to continue with this project.

To our neighbours for the many aperitif moments where I could vent and move forward. Thanks Inge and Yves! To our travel buddies Joris and Veronique who saw me disappear into the hammock in Tuscany several times to write some text, after which we toasted to friendship and the good life together.

To my close friends from Melsele (shout out to Orde der culinaire hoogmoed: Jan, Daan, Koen, Davy, Chris, Eli, Bram, Toon) and Mechelen for showing interest and providing support.

But the special thank you goes to Pieter Van Leugenhagen, a friend I've known for a very long time and who preceded me in writing a book ('Welcome to the Metaverse'). He gave me the proverbial push to start this book project. Thank you for sharing your knowledge and experience!

Shout out to my network!

This book would never have come to fruition without the support of my network. I would like to thank the following people. Firstly, the professional federations and their leaders who shared their insights with me: Lara Paemen (IFMA EMEA), Natalie Hofman (EuroFM / FMN), Ali Alsuwaidi (MEFMA), Alaa Alboali (MEFMA), Mark Whittaker (IWFM), Linda Hausmanis (IWFM), and Andrew Hulbert (IWFM). My colleagues from the board of IFMA Belgium for their support: Nathalie Cloet, Kris Cloots, Kristof Schrijvers, Isaac Eeckhout, Jan-Maarten Van Damme, Raf

Boterdaele, Joakim Van Gasse, Anton Maes, Lisa Mommaerts. And not to forget the other IFMA Chapters who introduced me to local experts: Kati Barklund (IFMA Sweden), Antti Pitkänen (IFMA Finland), Rebeca Fdez. Farpon (IFMA Spain).

The various use cases and experts I have had the pleasure to meet and get to know. This added so much value, not only to the book but also to myself as a person. Thank you for your valuable contribution: Pierrick Masure (Leesman), Sara De Oliveira (Accenture), Panos (Panagiotis) Machairas (ESA), Laurent Jauniaux (ESA), Ian Humphray (UCAS), Peter Ankerstjerne (Planon), Markus Sontheimer (ISS), Joy Trinquet (Verdantix), Rodolphe d'Arjuzon (Verdantix), Jan Nieuweboer (Rabo-bank), Jonas De Kerf (KUL), Paul Burgess (Aramco), Eddy Debrulle (Ageas), Ruud van der Sman (Edge), Andy van den Dobbelsteen (TU Delft), Danu Abesinghe (Le-novo), Etienne Friederichs (Facilicom), Eric Van Den Broele (GraydonCreditsafe), Tim Van Laere (GraydonCreditsafe), Hind Salhane (GraydonCreditsafe), Hind Murgab Mohamed Mahil, Mohamed Ibrahim Moursy Abdeldfattah (Etisalat FM), Niel Cortenraad, Mark van Haasteren (Vebego), Henrik Jarleskog (Sodexo), Erik Sörnäs (COOR), Fredrik Sandqvist (COOR), Jeff Dewing (Cloud FM), Jan Dunkelberg (Apleona), Tariq Chauhan (EFS), John Raspin (Frost&Sullivan), Jari Van Neyghem (BD), Koen Van Weyenbergh (BD), Renee Lefevre (BD), Vitalija Danivska (TU Delft), Hugo Mutsaerts (BUas), Sophie Vos (BUas), Annemarie Cortie (Facilicom), Mathi-as De Roeck (Unit-T), Rani Van Slembroeck (Vyncke), Jeffrey Saunders (Nordic Foresight), Hannah Wilson (LJMU), Matthew Tucker (LJMU), Ellen Daems (PRO-COS Group), Jos Duchamps (IFMA EMEA / PROCOS Group), Jean-Pierre Segers (Brains&Trees)

This book would never have come to fruition without my 'partner in crime', Stef Gyssels (ghostwriter). Thank you for wanting to accompany me on this enrich-ing journey! Thanks also to the publisher LannooCampus and Niels Janssens for believing in this project and giving me the opportunity to tell my story. Thank you Marije and Cami for your support during this process. And we must certainly not forget Ramon (you know who you are), who constantly forced us to critically question everything.

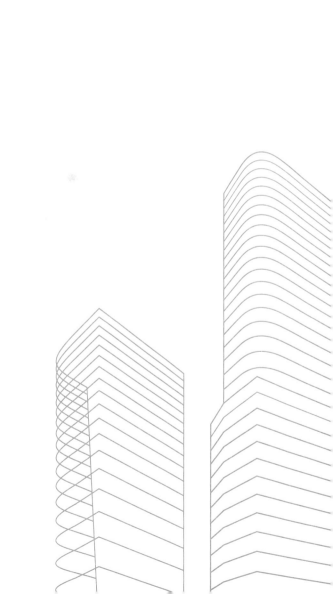

D/2024/45/74 – ISBN 978 94 014 0539 3 – NUR 800

Interior and cover design: Adept vormgeving

LannooCampus Publishers is a subsidiary of Lannoo Publishers, the book and multimedia division of Lannoo Publishers nv.

LannooCampus Publishers
Vaartkom 41 box 01.02   P.O. Box 23202
3000 Leuven   1100 DS Amsterdam
Belgium   The Netherlands
www.lannoocampus.com